Recipes, Restaurants, and Relationships
Defining Three Decades of
Sister City History

I0027700

The
CARMEL
kawachinagano
COOKBOOK

ETHan McAndrews

Illustrations by
Takeo Tsunamoto

BLUE
RIVER
PRESS

Indianapolis, Indiana

The Carmel Kawachinagano Cookbook: Recipes, Restaurants, and
Relationships Defining Three Decades of Sister City History
Copyright © 2025 by Ethan McAndrews

Published by Blue River Press
Indianapolis, Indiana
www.brpressbooks.com

Distributed by Cardinal Publishers Group
A Tom Doherty Company, Inc.
www.cardinalpub.com

All rights reserved under International and Pan-American
Copyright Conventions.

No part of this book may be reproduced, stored in a database or
other retrieval system, or transmitted in any form, by any means,
including mechanical, photocopy, recording or otherwise, without
the prior written permission of the publisher.

ISBN 978-1-68157-778-4

Cover Design: Anna Bovi
Book Design: Pei-Shing Chen
Editor: Chrissy Cutting
Illustrator: Takeo Tsunamoto

Printed in the United States of America

In memory of Aki Yamamoto and Jerry Myers

"Tell me what you eat, and I will tell you what you are."

- Jean Anthelme Brillat-Savarin

CONTENTS

FOREWORDS

Tomoaki Shimada
Mayor of Kawachinagano, 2016 – 2024

It was a pleasure to know Mr. Ethan McAndrews from Carmel. Ms. Lilia Shiba, President of KIFA (Kawachinagano International Friendship Association), and other members made all the necessary arrangements to support Ethan's research activities during his stay in our city. As Mayor of Kawachinagano, I felt that his stay in the city for several months produced a fruitful outcome for the two cities. I privately jogged with him a few times, and we enjoyed talking about the two cities, cultures, customs, economy, politics, and even gossip.

　カーメル出身のイーサン・マクアンドリュース氏と知り合えたことは喜ばしいことでした。KIFA（河内長野市国際交流協会）会長の柴理梨亜氏はじめ会員のみなさんは、当市滞在中のイーサン氏のリサーチ活動を支援するために必要なあらゆる手配をしました。河内長野市長として、彼の数ヶ月にわたる同市滞在が両市に実りある成果をもたらしたと感じています。個人的にも何度か彼とジョギングをし、両市のこと、文化、習慣、経済、政治、さらには噂話まで楽しく語り合うことができました。

Since establishing the sister city relationship between Carmel and Kawachinagano in 1994, the citizens of both cities have actively engaged in various exchanges. These include the exchange of fire and police department personnel, participation in the Carmel International Arts Festivals, and the exchange of artwork by school-children and students. Notably, both cities collaborated on the foundation of the Japanese garden on the premises next to Carmel City Hall. KIFA and Carmel Sister Cities, Inc. played an essential role in these activities, but the active participation of citizens made the exchange a success. In particular, I would like to mention the late Akihiko Yamamoto, the former president of KIFA, who passed away in 2023. Mr. Yamamoto served as president for sixteen years and was an unwavering supporter of the sister city relationship. Mr. Yamamoto also attended the twentieth anniversary ceremony in Carmel, when the Japanese garden was named Kawachinagano Japanese Garden. Thirty years is a long time, and we must remember many others who participated in our activities and supported us with their best efforts.

1994 年にカーメルと河内長野の姉妹都市関係が樹立されて以来、両市の市民は消防署員や警察署員の交換、カーメル国際アートフェスティバルへの参加、子ども絵画の交換など、さまざまな交流を積極的に行ってきました。特筆すべきは、両市が協力してカーメル市役所の隣接地に日本庭園を創設したことです。KIFA とカーメル姉妹都市委員会はこれらの活動で重要な役割を果たしましたが、成功は市民の積極的な参加によります。中でも 2023 年に亡くなった前会長の故山本明彦氏について触れておきたいと思います。山本氏は 16 年間 KIFA の会長を務め、姉妹都市関係の揺るぎない支持者でした。カーメルの日本庭園が河内長野日本庭園と命名された現地での 20 周年記念式典にも出席しました。30 年は長い年月であり、私たちの活動に参加し、最善を尽くして支援してくれた他の多くの人々を私たちは忘れてはなりません。

Five years ago, we erected a monument in the Kawachinagano City Hall premises to commemorate the twenty-fifth anniversary of our sister city relationship. The monument features a striking image of the Carmel Arts and Design District gate, symbolizing our shared cultural heritage. The logo plate of the Carmel Arts and Design District is right in the middle of the monument, giving the citizens of Kawachinagano a tangible connection to Carmel.

5年前、河内長野市役所敷地内に姉妹都市提携25周年を記念するモニュメントを建立しました。モニュメントはカーメルのアート＆デザイン地区の門を模し、共通の文化遺産を象徴しています。モニュメントの中央にはカーメルのアート＆デザイン地区のロゴプレートが置かれ、河内長野市民にカーメルとのつながりを実感させています。

This year, as we celebrate the thirtieth anniversary of the sister city relationship between Carmel and Kawachinagano, we look to the future with hope and excitement. To commemorate this milestone, a cookbook introducing the culinary cultures of the two cities is being published. This cookbook is not just a collection of recipes but a symbol of our shared values and the potential for further cultural exchange. It is a testament to our mutual understanding and respect for each other's cultures. I am confident that this cookbook will deepen our friendship and open a new chapter in developing our eternal bonds.

今年はカーメルと河内長野の姉妹都市提携 30 周年を迎え、私たちは希望と興奮を持って未来を見据えています。この節目を記念して、両市の食文化を紹介する料理本が出版されました。この料理本は、単なるレシピ集ではなく、共通の価値観とさらなる文化交流の可能性の象徴です。これは、私たちがお互いの文化を理解し、尊重し合っている証です。この料理本が私たちの友情を深め、永遠の絆を築く新たな章を開くものと確信しています。

Kawachinagano, Osaka, Japan
July 2024

Sue Finkam
Mayor of Carmel, 2024-Present

What does it take to be a good neighbor? That's a question that, by virtue of my position, I find myself asking quite often. Good neighbors are reliable. They're respectful. And, if you're out of town for the weekend, they may even collect a package or two. Carmel is full of these types of neighbors. We didn't elect or appoint them. They're just there, woven right into the fabric of our community. Because, ultimately, good neighbors make great neighborhoods, and great neighborhoods make world-class cities.

　良い隣人であるためには、何が必要でしょうか？ 私の立場上、この問いをよく考えることがあります。良い隣人とは、信頼できる人です。相手を尊重し、もしあなたが週末に留守にするなら、荷物を受け取ってくれるかもしれません。カーメル（Carmel）には、そんな隣人がたくさんいます。彼らは選挙で選ばれたり、任命されたりしたわけではありません。ただ、コミュニティの中に自然に溶け込んでいるのです。結局のところ、良い隣人が素晴らしい近隣を作り、素晴らしい近隣が世界に誇る街を作るのです。

But the need for good neighbors does not cease at Carmel's city limits. As we work tirelessly toward the prosperity of our home, we must remember the relationships we've forged with Carmel's sister cities—our international neighbors.

しかし、良い隣人の必要性は、カーメル市の境界線で止まるものではありません。そして、私たちが自分たちの街の繁栄のために懸命に働く中で、カーメルの姉妹都市、つまり私たちの国際的な隣人たちとの関係も忘れてはなりません。

The city has welcomed five new sister cities in the past three years. Altogether, we have six such relationships. The neighborhood is growing. What will it take to be a good international neighbor? More than package pick-ups, clearly. It will take people like Ethan McAndrews, Takeo Tsunamoto, and the staff of the Kawachinagano International Friendship Association (KIFA). It will take public officials like Jim Brainard, Tomoaki Shimada, and Shuhei Nishino. And it will take projects like The Carmel-Kawachinagano Cookbook.

この3年間で、カーメル市は新たに5つの姉妹都市を迎え入れました。合計で6つの姉妹都市関係を持っています。この「近隣」は成長しています。では、良い国際的な隣人であるためには、何が必要でしょうか？それは、荷物の受け取り以上のものです。例

えば、イーサン・マクアンドリューズ（Ethan McAndrews）氏、
綱本武雄（Takeo Tsunamoto）氏、そして河内長野市国際交
流協会（KIFA）のスタッフのような人々が必要です。また、ジ
ム・ブレイナード（Jim Brainard）市長、島田智明（Tomoaki
Shimada）市長、西野修平（Shuhei Nishino）氏のような公
務員も必要です。そして、「カーメル・河内長野クックブック（The
Carmel-Kawachinagano Cookbook）」のようなプロジェクトも
必要です。

When I assumed office in January 2024, I did not anticipate my
portfolio would include organizing the publication of a cookbook.
But then I talked with Ethan McAndrews, and I knew this project
would be much more than a few flashy recipes. Ethan is a good
neighbor. He's smart, passionate, and most importantly, dedicated
to telling the human stories that connect Carmel to Kawachinagano, 6,550 miles away.

　2024年1月に就任した際、私の職務の中に料理本の出版を企
画することが含まれるとは思っていませんでした。しかし、イーサン・
マクアンドリューズ氏と話をしたとき、このプロジェクトが単なる派
手なレシピ集以上のものであることを確信しました。イーサン氏は
良い隣人です。彼は賢く、情熱的で、何よりも、6,550マイル離
れたカーメルと河内長野をつなぐ人間味あふれる物語を伝えること
に専念しています。

And across the Pacific, the support from Kawachinagano on this project has reinforced my commitment to deep, meaningful collaboration between our two cities. From Takeo Tsunamoto, the cookbook's illustrator, to KIFA and the officials at Kawachinagano City Hall, I'm inspired by the rich spirit of exchange that runs through this project.

そして太平洋を越え、このプロジェクトに対する河内長野市からのサポートは、私が両市間の深く意味のある協力関係を推進したいという思いをさらに強めました。イラストレーターの綱本氏から、KIFA、そして河内長野市役所の職員に至るまで、このプロジェクトに流れる豊かな交流の精神には感銘を受けます。

It's clear that Carmel's thriving relationship with Kawachinagano is a testament to good neighbors. For the past thirty years, our two cities have worked together to promote mutual understanding, cultural dialogue, and educational exchange. And these contributions are worth celebrating. However, once the celebrations end, we must turn our attention to the next thirty years of sister city collaboration. There are new technologies to leverage, new communities to reach, and new opportunities to explore. I'm confident we can continue to serve as a leading example of international exchange. Why? Because our cities are full of good neighbors—local people who work together to create something special, like The Carmel-Kawachinagano Cookbook.

カーメル市と河内長野市の活気ある関係は、良い隣人の存在を示す証です。この 30 年間、私たちの両市は相互理解、文化的対話、教育交流を促進するために協力してきました。そして、これらの貢献は称賛に値します。しかし、祝賀が終わった後は、姉妹都市としての次の 30 年に目を向けなければなりません。新しい技術を活用し、新しいコミュニティに手を差し伸べ、新たな機会を探求する必要があります。私は、私たちが引き続き国際交流の模範となり続けることに自信があります。なぜなら、私たちの街には良い隣人がたくさんいるからです。彼らは、「カーメル・河内長野クックブック」のような特別なものを共に創り上げるために協力している地元の人々なのです。

Carmel, Indiana, USA
January 2025

PREFACE

1. WHAT IS THIS BOOK ABOUT?

It's about two sister cities, Carmel and Kawachinagano, and what people eat there. The writing comes from my time living in Carmel and visiting Kawachinagano twice. I spent most of my time in the Osaka suburbs living with families and eating meals that seemed too beautiful for me to eat. I took 2,237 photos and logged twenty-three hours of voice memos.

I struggle to name a genre for this book. In the title, I refer to it as a cookbook—the term by this point is a type of shorthand to friends for the physical and emotional toll of this writing endeavor. There are recipes, almost thirty of them, so the book surely clears some low-hanging threshold of the cookbook genre.

There's another side of me that wants to call this a travelogue. It's the side that admires Anthony Bourdain, speaks Mandarin, and collects passport stamps. But saying I wrote a travelogue feels like calling Cheez Whiz and crackers an *amuse-bouche*—it's wrong, pretentious, and ultimately obfuscates more than it reveals. I did travel to Kawachinagano for four months, though—and then I wrote about it. Within those chapters, there is a thread of travelogue-like discovery, one which I tried to extend through the Carmel side of my writing, too.

Almost every chapter is about a different person, restaurant, or dish that reveals something about Kawachinagano or Carmel.

They are less chapters and more profiles. There are recurring characters and settings, but my goal is that you can read this cookbook/travelogue/whatever in any sequence you want. Each chapter should feel like looking through a periscope—you can peer around the corner and catch a glimpse of someone's far-off life. And ideally, after enough glimpses, our cities will cease to be abstracts and turn into real places with people and food and laughter and hope.

2. WHY FOOD?

Because everyone eats. Most people eat the same, really, despite different cultures and climates. There are proteins, carbs, fats, and vegetables in almost every kitchen on earth. I'm not out to prove Indiana's pork tenderloin is the same as Japan's pork katsu. But ultimately, those dishes have a common denominator: crispy, golden, deep-fried pork. If you like tenderloin and I like katsu, we already know something about each other—all without buying a plane ticket or pocket translator. We speak a common language.

Food is also this weird dichotomy of universal and personal. A phrase like "everyone eats" can imply two very different things. First, that all eight billion of us, regardless of gender, race, religion, etc., consume food. Eating is a biological requirement for survival. And second, "everyone eats" can mean each individual person eats. Picture the person across from you eating their lunch. Are they sitting down, standing—driving? Are they scrolling through their phone? How are they chewing? It's hard not to sketch an intimate picture.

This book should really be about culture. It's just that my limited stabs at detailing local culture either read like a tourism pamphlet or an academic proposal. Food is intuitive, immediate. I could describe the Buddhist influences of Kongō-ji Temple— I could even show you photos on my phone—but there's no manual for how to build your own at home. The first time you try the recipe for curry rice or taste Bosco Sticks, you'll get a real glimpse of what it's like to live in these cities.

One last note about food, what this book is or isn't, and how it's organized. I don't think this book is about Japanese or Indiana cuisine. Even the term "Indiana cuisine" sounds flat and formal. I tried to write, as Chef Jason Crouch put it, about food with first names: the people who make it and the people who eat it— characters, like any good story must have. There's a butcher, a baker, and a barista. There's a mom, a fishmonger—the same woman, actually—lots of farmers, an innkeeper, a few chefs, and a city hall official. There's a high school teacher and his former student and *his* former student.

I've organized the recipes by mealtime because that's how I encountered them. That's how people ate them. Cuisines are great, but I leave that to the professionals. This is ultimately a collection of stories about meals I shared at specific times with specific people.

3. DO YOU SPEAK JAPANESE?

No.

3.a. ISN'T THAT KIND OF PROBLEMATIC WHEN YOU'RE WRITING A BOOK ABOUT JAPANESE FOOD AND CULTURE?

Maybe. I don't know. I'm less concerned about this whole thing being problematic than I am about the types of things I may have overlooked because I don't speak Japanese.

I will say I don't think this project would have been successful if I had known Japanese beforehand. Part of this was me trying to encounter Kawachinagano for the first time. If I had studied Japanese previously, or even visited Japan prior to writing, I'd be missing something—a struggle that makes the work significantly more real.

Adjusting to life in Kawachinagano also forced me to confront challenges I'd probably skate past if it was my fifth or sixth time in-country. I can still tell you every station on the Nankai-Koya line between Kawachinagano and Osaka City. Not because I'm really smart or love commuter transit, but because I missed my stop every day for the first month. And that's okay—the struggle was necessary. Lacking proficient Japanese, I couldn't help but hang on all the small, silent cues that provided context to life in Kawachinagano. And I had my excuse to take an obnoxious number of notes.

It's important to add that my whole wide-eyed approach was buttressed by KIFA's incredibly generous translation help, specifically Harumi Goto. For several months, and on almost a daily basis, KIFA turned my colloquial, Midwest ramblings into coherent Japanese. I cannot emphasize how consistently and thoroughly they saved me, my reputation, and this book throughout the research process.

4. WHAT/WHO IS KIFA?

KIFA stands for Kawachinagano International Friendship Association. It's the organization responsible for this book. It's independent, volunteer-based, and gets its funding from Kawachinagano City Hall. The mandate on KIFA's homepage is broad:

To foster international awareness among Kawachinagano citizens to fulfill the needs of a multicultural society.

That covers everything from intermediate Korean classes to Halloween trick-or-treating at the public library. There are two full-time staff members: Tadashi Yamamoto and Megumi Kinoshita. KIFA also has a few long-haul volunteers: Shiba-san, Goto-san, Hiroko-san, Ueda-san, and Yuki-san. All of us drove out to Kansai Airport together on the morning of my departure. More than half cried.

5. WHAT WAS YOUR RESEARCH PROCESS LIKE?

A lot of listening and asking questions and patience. Almost every good idea or recipe in here started out as a coffee chat or Zoom call. I had my own vision, especially for the Carmel side, but I wanted to keep the content flexible and focus on structure and style rather than specific recipes. I read a lot, too. Cookbooks, textbooks, memoirs—whatever I could find on food, travel, and writing about those two devotions at the same time.

I don't want to use a word like experiential, but that's really how the research went. I'd learn about a pear farm, go talk to the farmer, and then write about it. Whenever I strayed from that process, like if I tried to write about a meal I saw in a viral video, the product felt stale. Honestly, and I'm conscious not to lean too heavily into food analogies here, it felt like reheating leftovers in a microwave.

I also found a direct correlation between the quality of my research and the depth of my listening. I've known this rule for a while now. But once I started interviewing locals in Kawachinagano, *quality = depth* became my survival guide. I didn't have a set framework. Usually, I'd look around and not say much and let the other person talk as much as they wanted. This was mostly out of humility. I wasn't about to show up to the noodle shop assuming I knew the best way to make udon. But I also took this approach because it worked. My best interviews were 80-20: I asked questions 20 percent of the time and shut up for the other 80 percent. The food helped. I became world-class at firing questions off right before taking a prolonged bite.

On my first full day in Kawachinagano, I sat down with KIFA and planned out all three months' worth of interviews. Seriously, we booked a conference room and didn't leave until we finalized the entire schedule, day-by-day, week-by-week. The whole thing gave me a glimpse of KIFA's status in Kawachinagano.

It would go like this: Shiba-san would ask what type of features I wanted to include in the book. At least one farm, I'd say. And then someone, usually Hiroko-san, would pull out a cell phone, make a quick call—nodding and laughing the whole time in a way that made it obvious, even in one-sided Japanese, that the person on the other line was totally charmed—and suddenly we'd have our farm visit lined up for 10 a.m. on October 18. There was no one we couldn't reach.

6. HOW DO YOU PRONOUNCE KAWACHINAGANO?

I've heard plenty of variations. Some are hushed and unsure. Others should be but are not. Here's the general rule:

Kawachinagano is the composite name of several villages that combined in 1954: Nagano, Mikkaichi, Kawakami, Amami, Kagata, and Tako. Nagano is easy—it's pronounced "Nah Gah No." Kawachi, a composite of the other villages, is pronounced "Kah Wah Chee."

Altogether, it sounds like "Kahwachee Nahgahno."

7. OKAY, BUT WHAT IS JAPAN REALLY LIKE?

I don't know. I lived there for eight months, and I barely glimpsed it. I caught a thousand little details and interactions that felt loosely tied to some collective way of doing things, but, as individual moments, they seemed fleeting, ordinary, and underwhelming. None have the anecdotal firepower to package the whole country into a good line here. Damn. All I can tell you is that Japan, like most everywhere, is trying its best. It has its unique history, challenges, and aspirations. People there are thoughtful and earnest. And the trains are nearly perfect.

A QUICK NOTE ABOUT NAMES AND PRONUNCIATIONS

Many of the Japanese names in this book read with the suffix -san. For example, Tsunamoto-san or Takeo-san instead of Tsunamoto or just Takeo. That's the polite way of referring to someone—both in written reference and conversation. The English equivalent is Mr. and Mrs. Furthermore, the order of given names and family names is the reverse of English, so Takeo's first name appears after his family name, Tsunamoto. Throughout the book, I've tried to present people in the manner I knew them. So my original host parents, the Tsunamotos, are Takeo-san and Koto-san. KIFA's Secretary General, Yamamoto Tadashi, is Yamamoto-san.

I've italicized Japanese terms that appear in English, where relevant. There is no single standard of romanization, and for the sake of accessibility, my approach is a really basic one. Terms like *ryokan* (旅館), the traditional Japanese-style inn, appear simply as ryokan. Letters that have distinct pronunciations, like the e at the end of *sake*, are marked accordingly. The e is pronounced like the French word exposé or *bebé*.

PROLOGUE

If you tell someone you're going to Japan, and they've been to Japan, they will give you advice. I received a great deal. So much so that it almost took on a rhythmic quality, like a steady countdown to my departure flight. Make business cards, people said, it's a big business card culture. I read whole email threads with subject lines like "DOMO ARIGATO!" explaining the difference between Kansai and Kanto. I learned how to give a good gift and how to receive a bad one. Did I know if my chargers worked in Japan? Yes, Google said they would.

So it was almost funny, with the small travel agency's worth of advice I received, that my undoing would be distinctly American. I could name the entire Imperial Family. I knew Kanto was more cosmopolitan than Kansai. I even knew the Boss Coffee logo was supposed to be Tommy Lee Jones. I did not know, however, how to make apple pie. This was never really an issue until 9:00 a.m. on Saturday, December 3, 2023—formally advertised as "Saturday Morning Apple Pie Class with Ethan McAndrews in KICCS 4th Floor Teaching Kitchen."

Dwight Eisenhower is responsible for my all-American undoing. In 1956, Eisenhower launched his "citizen diplomacy" initiative from the White House, encouraging communities across America to deepen their international ties. Cities and towns started looking for cultural, linguistic, and economic counterparts around the world.

Eventually, Eisenhower's vision for citizen-to-citizen exchange spurred the creation of formal sister cities. Indianapolis and Cologne, Germany are sister cities, for example. So are New York City and Madrid. These ties often materialize from common interests—in the case of Indy and Cologne, an artistic exchange between the Indianapolis Museum of Art and the Wallraf-Richartz Museum in Cologne.

As of this writing, Carmel has six sister cities: Kawachinagano, Japan; Jelgava, Latvia; Cortona, Italy; Seiffen, Germany; Visakhapatnam, India; and Rueil-Malmaison, France. Kawachinagano is the longest running by several decades. After a successful exchange program between Kawachinagano's Seikyo Gakuen and Carmel High School, the southern Osaka city finalized its formal relationship with Carmel on April 8, 1994.

So while Eisenhower didn't directly push me into the pie-making class, he'd probably enjoy it. My trip to Japan, like this cookbook, was a product of citizen diplomacy. The weeks proceeded smoothly until KIFA mistook my love of eating food as a talent for making it. I got an apron, an ingredient list, and a prime-time slot on Saturday morning.

I showed up twenty minutes before the class and refreshed "How to Make Apple Pie From Scratch Easy Simple" on YouTube. KIFA had configured the kitchen into a chemistry lab, with multiple stovetops across the classroom and a long, rectangular countertop designating the instructor's station. Soon, families began finding their seats. Someone switched my soft rock to a Christmas playlist for a "better classroom atmosphere." The right call, looking back.

The class started off great. Zero cuts, fires, or allergic reactions. I was three steps away from finishing the whole thing when I realized my mistake. No sugar. Even with limited YouTube prep, I knew sugar wasn't optional. I improvised, telling my class to sprinkle the sugar over their apples like a Christmas snowfall. They sprinkled, we latticed our pies, and everything worked out fine. KIFA even intervened with a scoop of ice cream to smooth out my mistakes.

That morning, I realized two things: If you wear an apron and talk with your hands and stand behind a big, restaurant-grade countertop, people will think you know how to bake a pie. The class didn't flinch when I eyeballed out the pie dough or pulverized a stick of butter. It was a commanding feeling. I get why Rachel Ray does it.

I also stopped to consider the whole span of events tha led to my pie-making debut. (Literally, as in I stopped baking for a second and questioned how I ended up in that classroom, in that city, writing this cookbook.)

Sister cities are beautiful things. They cut through politics and bureaucracy and get straight to the personal, small-town realities that are almost impossible to glean from newspaper headlines. Most, like Carmel and Kawachinagano, are not flashy. But they are the best way to understand a place. A real, local community of people—not a prefecture or a country.

Because of their nature, sister cities are also fragile. They rely on everyday people operating without institutional budgets, language training, or diplomatic attachés. I got to Kawachinagano because seven or eight people, most of whom work separate full-time jobs, believed in the importance of bringing our two cities together. They believed enough to bridge a 6,550-mile gap and organize all the stressful details of my three-month stay in Japan.

Not all of this came to mind during the second I stopped baking. But my struggle with apple pie is sort of the perfect image for maintaining a sister city. I assumed baking the pie was going to be easy. The ingredients are simple enough—apples, butter, flour, sugar— and the steps follow logically. It turns out baking is decisively not easy. Instructions that read like English conceal layers of chemistry and calculus. There's timing and heat and precision and hundreds of other variables that can sabotage the whole dessert. Baking apple pie may be simple, but it's not easy.

Just like Carmel and Kawachinagano. Building up a sister city relationship, especially between two small communities, is simple. There are a couple of important dates to remember, and every few years, we host a delegation. Our mayors, should crisis arise, can WhatsApp each other. But there's nothing easy about doing that for thirty years—maintaining, growing, and ultimately, passing down a bond like that over generations.

It's tempting to view thirty years of momentum as a sign of self-sufficiency, to find the ingredients already in the bowl and walk away satisfied. But sister cities will always need people from across the world—most of whom will never meet—to care about friendship, community, and, most importantly, one another. No, it's not easy—it's simple. And repetitive. And meaningful.

September 2024
Carmel, Indiana

Me and Takeo-san on the first day we met. And chibi.

BREAKFAST

TAMAGOYAKI

A translation like "omelet" fails to capture the intricacy of tama-goyaki. It sounds simple enough at first. *Tamago* means egg. *Yaki* describes something grilled or pan-fried over heat. But the complexity comes in the preparation—in how the *tamago* is *yaki'd*, you could say. Tamagoyaki is a scramble of egg, sugar, and special stock called dashi poured into a square-shaped pan, rolled, and then rolled several more times. The burrito-shaped roll of egg batter is then wedged and served cold, usually with a small side of grated radish.

I ate lots of tamagoyaki throughout my stay in Kawachinagano. It's a simple, filling dish— I never thought much of it. But then I met Aya Miyazaki and her family.

Aya-san runs a small bentō restaurant from her family kitchen, about three miles south of City Hall. I spent two days living with the Miyazakis. By the time I woke up and organized my futon bedding, Aya-san was already busy organizing the kitchen into several culinary prep stations. Her husband,

Daisuke-san, would make a quick pour-over coffee and catch the bus to Osaka for work. Then the kids, Kotaro and Konatsu, would come running down the stairs, half-dressed for school. It was a familiar type of functioning chaos. I immediately felt at home.

Tamagoyaki is eaten at breakfast and lunch. In the latter case, it's usually featured in bentō, the classic box-style lunch enjoyed by schoolchildren and salarymen alike. It's never the main star of the box—a role typically reserved for sashimi or tempura—but it's always a reliable bite. The rolled egg is dense and custardy, with a warm sweetness from the sugar.

Back at the Miyazakis' home, I watched Aya-san pour the egg batter into her square pan. Cook, roll, oil, repeat. The intricacy of the dish requires patience—the same type of patience one learns from early school-day mornings and piling lunch orders. In both regards, Aya-san is a pro. She makes the tamagoyaki to prove it.

TAMAGOYAKI

(Makes 1 roll)

INGREDIENTS

- 4 eggs
- 5 tbsp. dashi stock
- 1 tsp. sugar
- 1 tbsp. light soy sauce
- 1 tbsp. oil (for pan)

INSTRUCTIONS

① Scramble eggs in a medium-sized bowl. Add additional ingredients and mix thoroughly.

② Warm omelet pan to medium-high heat and coat with oil.

③ Ladle a thin layer of egg mixture into the pan. Once the mixture sets, begin rolling it towards you from the far edge of the pan.

④ Re-oil pan and repeat step three until the mixture is cooked.

⑤ Cut the cooked roll into equal pieces (approx. 6) and serve.

WHITE RICE & MISO SOUP

Some foods just belong together. They form a bond that can't exist separately, like two magnets crashing into each other. The list is long: bacon and eggs, milk and cookies, peanut butter and jelly, etc. But there's another duo that deserves just as much respect, if not more: white rice and miso soup.

The humble pairing defines food culture in Japan. White rice and miso soup work together like two delicious, interlocking puzzle pieces. And nowhere is the magic more obvious than at the breakfast table.

Steak and potatoes rarely makes the menu. Breakfast in Kawachinagano features tea, pickled vegetables (*tsukemono*), and steamed white rice next to a bowl of miso soup. Maybe a side of salt-cured salmon, if you're lucky. At its most basic, the meal is pared down to two bowls and a pair of chopsticks—you drink the miso soup directly.

How did this duo come to dominate breakfast in Japan? The answer is part history, part gastronomy, and part biology.

The origins of Japanese food culture point to the phrase *ichiju-san-sai* ("one soup, three side dishes"). Side dishes varied over time—sometimes pickled radish, sometimes dried fish—but rice and miso soup remained constant for thousands of years. Large-scale rice farming began in Japan during the Yayoi period in 500 BC. Buddhist priests from China introduced miso to Japan in the late sixth century AD. By the start of the Edo period (1603–1867), the two foods had become staples nationwide. And the tradition lives on today. Over 80 percent of Japan's population eats rice every day, and 75 percent drink miso soup.

The flavor helps, of course. The exact taste defies English vocabulary, or, at least, my own, but Japanese offers the precise word: umami. The term refers to rich, deep flavors—think slow-roasted pork, bone broth, or a dark, rich tomato. Today, experts recognize umami as a distinct, taste-bud-certified flavor alongside saltiness, sweetness, bitterness, and sourness.

But the magic of this partnership goes beyond history and taste. There's science at play here, too. Miso paste is fermented, meaning it feeds on bacteria as it ages. The paste consists of salt, mashed soybeans, and a mold known as koji (or *aspergillus oryzae*, if your Latin is better than your Japanese). The resulting mix is sealed and left to ferment anywhere from several months to multiple years. Why is all this important? Miso contains key enzymes that break down complex starches—the same complex starches you'd find, for example, in a bowl of white rice. The breakfast duo is not just delicious but compatible on a molecular scale. Your move, bacon and eggs.

BISCUITS & GRAVY

Breakfast in Carmel is rarely a luxurious affair. During the week, it's a rushed grab at countertop toast, washed down with a hot coffee and promptly forgotten. What does luxury look like, then? Free of work, school, and other early morning obligations, what's on the menu?

I visited Carmel's Sunrise Cafe early one August morning to find out. The cafe is tucked alongside a sprawling office complex off 116th Street and Meridian. Even at 7:45 a.m., the parking lot was already full of corporate employees, ties-donned, eyes slightly dead, very clearly not headed for a long, sit-down breakfast. I shuffled through a crowd of briefcases to the cafe's front door.

Sunrise Cafe has the distinct, unflashy charm of a restaurant that's been part of the Carmel community since 1985. There is no urgency to impress or persuade. The food has passed the test of time; anything left to prove is communicated directly through the menu.

I walked through the entryway and settled into a booth on the edge of the carpeted dining area. The nearby tables were full—mostly men in shades of business casual drinking coffee. They rotated in and out on half-hour blocks, like a real-time Google Calendar. I was here strictly for leisure, however. More specifically, I was here for a comfort food classic: biscuits and gravy. I ordered, sipped my refill of black coffee, and waited.

Sunrise Cafe opens at 6:00 a.m. every morning. The owner, Jim Horsfield, is usually in by 5:00 a.m. His philosophy on the restaurant business hasn't changed since 1985: Every day is a new start. It's a Sisyphean mindset that requires discipline and a good alarm clock. Still, even if each day starts at zero, the years add up.

Sunrise Cafe is the morning person's breakfast spot in Carmel. It was easy to see why, too, as my waitress returned less than ten minutes later with a bowl of hot gravy flanked by two fresh biscuits.

I am by no means a technical expert of proper B&G technique. The breakfast community itself is split. Do you pour the gravy over the biscuits and cut as you go or slice the biscuits open first, sandwich style, for wider gravy application? I'd say just do whatever feels right. Dip the biscuits milk-and-cookie style if you want. As long as the gravy is creamy and the biscuits are fluffy, you've already won. Remember, this is a leisurely breakfast.

BISCUITS & GRAVY

(Makes 6 servings)

INGREDIENTS

- ○ 2 cups all-purpose flour
- ○ 1 tablespoon baking powder
- ○ 1/2 teaspoon baking soda
- ○ 1 teaspoon salt
- ○ 6 tablespoons cold unsalted butter, cubed
- ○ 4/3 cup cold buttermilk

For the Sausage Gravy

- ○ 1 pound breakfast sausag
- ○ 1/4 cup all-purpose flour
- ○ 2 1/2 cups whole milk
- ○ 1/2 teaspoon salt
- ○ 1/2 teaspoon black pepper

INSTRUCTIONS

① Preheat oven to 425° F. In a large bowl, whisk together flour, baking powder, baking soda, and salt.

② Cut in butter using a pastry cutter or fork until the mixture resembles coarse crumbs. Pour in buttermilk and stir until just combined.

③ Turn dough onto a floured surface and gently pat into a 3/4-inch thick rectangle. Cut into biscuits using a round cutter or a knife.

④ Place on a parchment-lined baking sheet and bake for 12-15 minutes, or until golden brown.

⑤ In a large skillet over medium heat, cook the sausage, breaking it up as it browns. Sprinkle flour over the sausage and stir for 1-2 minutes until absorbed.

⑥ Gradually pour in milk, stirring constantly, until thickened. Season with salt and black pepper.

⑤ Split biscuits and ladle gravy over the top. Serve warm.

LIEGE WAFFLES

The best way to find The Walking Waffle Co. at the Carmel Farmers Market is to look for a line. And not just any line—usually, the longest one, wrapped around a few brick-paved corners, full of strollers, couples, and hungry families. Once you find it, just get in. The waffle is worth it.

The Walking Waffle Co. began in 2008 as a way for Mark and Stephanie Lewis to pass down the value of hard work and community to their four kids. Today, the family business has expanded to five farmers markets in Indiana, an online store, and Carmel's annual Christkindlmarkt. Shelby Lewis, who started as a young waffle-making assistant, runs the show with her husband, Parker Lorch.

Back to the Saturday morning line. The further along you shuffle, the more you see (and smell) why families will wait twenty-five minutes in the Midwest summer heat for a waffle. An assembly line begins to take shape. Prep stations are meticulous and, in true family-run style, staffed by a brigade of siblings, relatives, and friends.

My personal favorite is the classic: a fresh Liege (Belgian) waffle topped with blueberries and whipped cream. The dough, with its signature baked-in sugar crystals, is decadently rich. The toppings provide a fresh, aesthetically pleasing balance. It's a delicious combo and, more importantly, a treat worth almost any wait.

LIEGE WAFFLES

(Makes about 8 waffles)

INGREDIENTS

- 3 1/2 cups all-purpose flour
- 1 packet (2 1/4 tsp) active dry yeast
- 1/2 cup warm milk
- 2 large eggs
- 1 teaspoon vanilla extract
- 1 teaspoon salt
- 2 tablespoons brown sugar
- 1 cup unsalted butter, softened
- 1 1/2 cups pearl sugar

INSTRUCTIONS

1. Dissolve yeast in warm milk and let sit for 5-10 minutes until foamy.
2. In a large bowl, mix flour, eggs, vanilla, salt, and brown sugar.
3. Pour in yeast mixture and stir until a sticky dough forms.
4. Knead in softened butter a little at a time until fully incorporated.
5. Cover and let dough rise in a warm place for 1 1/2 to 2 hours, or until doubled in size.
6. Gently fold in pearl sugar, then divide dough into 8 equal pieces.
7. Preheat waffle iron to medium heat and lightly grease.
8. Cook each dough ball in the waffle iron for 3-5 minutes until golden brown and caramelized.
9. Let cool slightly before serving.

POUR-OVER COFFEE

The perfect pour-over is a balancing act. It's algorithmic, on one hand. There are timed intervals and bean-to-water ratios and precision scales that read to the one-thousandth of a gram. Verbs like tare are thrown around casually.

But a pour-over is also distinctly personal. Literally, as in you do the pouring-over. There is no La Marzocco to bail you out, no warm blanket of milk to soften a crash landing. The final result is like a handwriting sample: both reflective and revealing of its author.

Your pour-over's fate is in your barista's hands.

There are also the hands themselves. Pour-overs are also known as "hand-drips," referring to the technique of manually pouring hot water over ground coffee. The hands set the variables—speed, direction, volume—that collide and ultimately determine the cup's quality. The fate of your pour-over, in a very real sense, is in your barista's hands.

This all feels especially fitting as I watch my mom work behind the counter at Indie Coffee Roasters. She would tell you that algorithms aren't omnipotent and that good coffee is made more with feeling than fact. (She'd find a better word than "omnipotent.") She can say this, seven years after opening ICR's first shop in Carmel, because her hands have memorized the math. Her fingertips track time, and her wrists set the tempo. Which, in turn, leaves her mind free to engage an archive of its own: the names, jobs, families, hopes, and dreams of every customer sitting at the counter.

My dear own personal mom runs Indie Coffee Roasters the same way she raised children. She's kind, thoughtful, and relentless in both worlds. Regulars see the parallels, too, in the small ways the shop feels like Carmel's living room. She remembers names, celebrates birthdays, and hugs with a closeness generally reserved for family. On some level, when you're in the shop, you're family, too.

LUNCH

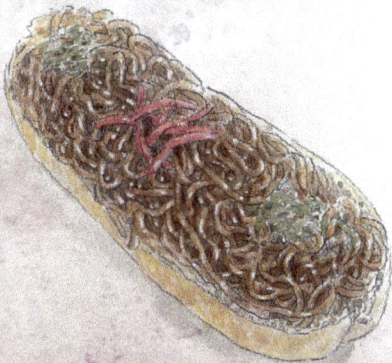

SOBA

There's almost no such thing as too much soba. It's a versatile noodle—healthier than ramen and heartier than udon. It's fast, too. The term "standing soba" comes from the countless noodle shops around train stations across Japan. Busy commuters will pop into closet-sized shops, slurp down a bowl of the brown buckwheat noodles, and head on their way. No words or chairs required.

My elderly soba-making instructor in Kawachinagano swore by the noodle's health properties. When I met him, he was riding a twelve-year streak of soba every day for lunch. "It's good for the heart," he told me.

I believed him—and not just because he was nimble with the rolling pin. Soba fills you up. It's earthy, nutty, and just a little firm. The noodles are distinctly thin, almost like spaghetti, with a different taste and texture.

1. 混ぜる / Mix   2. こねる / Knead   3. 圧す / Flat

4. 折る / Fold

そば包丁 / Soba knife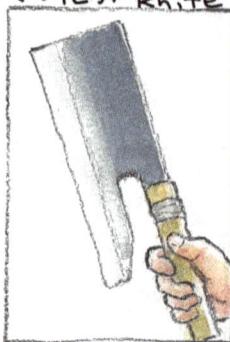

5. 切る / Cut

6. ゆでる / Boil

7. 洗う / Cool

I eat my soba cold, with a sprinkle of soy sauce and green onions. My noodle sensei preferred it hot, served in a soup-like broth called dashi. You can even pan-fry the noodles and top them with a fried egg. The odds are that whatever combination you choose will be healthy, filling, and, most importantly, delicious.

SOBA

(Makes about 4 servings)

INGREDIENTS

○ 2 cups (240g) buckwheat flour

○ 1/2 cup (60g) all-purpose flour (or more buckwheat flour for gluten-free)

○ 1/2 cup (120ml) cold water (adjust as needed)

○ Extra flour (for dusting)

INSTRUCTIONS

① In a large bowl, mix buckwheat flour and all-purpose flour.

② Slowly add cold water, mixing with hands until a rough dough forms.

③ Knead for about 10 minutes until smooth and firm. If too dry, add a teaspoon of water at a time.

④ Wrap the dough in plastic wrap and let it rest for 30 minutes.

⑤ Lightly flour a surface and roll out the dough into a thin sheet (about 1/8 inch thick).

⑥ Fold the dough in thirds, then slice into thin strips (about 1/8 inch wide).

⑦ Boil a large pot of water and cook noodles for 1-2 minutes. Drain and rinse under cold water to remove excess starch.

TONKATSU

After a full month in Japan, I started to miss home. Nothing overwhelming, but a real longing for something Midwestern and familiar. Harumi-san and Megumi-san sensed this, I'm convinced, because they both grinned as we walked into a local tonkatsu shop for lunch. Almost immediately, my eyes caught a display case near the entryway: five glistening, deep-fried cutlets illuminated behind glass like rare museum jewels. Fried pork tenderloins. Was this Carmel or Kawachinagano?

Tonkatsu cured my homesickness. Or, at the very least, it made Japan look a little more like home. That lunch felt more like finding a long-lost relative than trying a new dish. It tasted more like State Fair, USA, than Kawachinagano, Japan.

The twin-like similarity between Japan's tonkatsu and Indiana's pork tenderloin sandwich has a history. Tonkatsu emerged with Japan's push for greater meat consumption during the Meiji era (1868–1912). Rapid modernization mixed—not always peacefully—with Western influence and spurred new hybrids of Japanese food. When the French introduced *porc côtelette* (think pork chop) around Tokyo in the 1890s, Japanese chefs responded by egg-battering and tempura-frying the new cutlet, undoubtedly pissing off *les cuisiniers*. Lines grew, and soon the breaded, deep-fried tonkatsu emerged as a staple of Japanese comfort food.

The pork tenderloin sandwich's origin story is strikingly similar: a European import at the turn of the twentieth century analyzed, localized, and commercialized by resourceful locals. Taxonomically, the two dishes are different species of the same genus. Put very not taxonomically, tonkatsu is like the P.T. Sandwich's worldly cousin who moved to Tokyo and opened a kickass jazz club.

Tonkatsu, in another break from its Hoosier relative, rarely comes with calorie-packed sides. Its only complement is a reliable heap of shredded cabbage, a side that serves as much aesthetically as it does functionally. My cutlet looked healthier with a side of greens. It tasted lighter, too. Harumi-san and Megumi-san insisted that cabbage helped digestion and prevented post-lunch heartburn. I noted the dietary potential for Indiana's pork tenderloin culture.

The word tonkatsu can be deconstructed as *ton* (pork) and *katsu* (cutlet). But *katsu* here sounds identical to the Japanese verb "to win." And, like most superstitions, sometimes, a convincing homonym is all you need. Tonkatsu shops are careful pilgrimages for students studying for a final exam or businessmen preparing for an investment pitch.

A few weeks after my first cutlet, I landed an interview for a part-time summer job. I immediately booked another lunch before my call. I'm not superstitious, but I'll take any excuse to eat tonkatsu.

TONKATSU

INGREDIENTS

- ○ 2 boneless pork chops (1/2 – 3/4 inch thick)
- ○ 1/2 teaspoon salt
- ○ 1/4 teaspoon black pepper
- ○ 1/4 cup all-purpose flour
- ○ 1 egg, beaten
- ○ 1/2 cup panko breadcrumbs
- ○ 1 cup vegetable oil (for frying)

INSTRUCTIONS

1. Lightly pound pork chops to an even thickness. Season both sides with salt and pepper.

2. Dredge each cutlet in flour, then dip in beaten egg, and coat evenly with panko breadcrumbs.

3. Heat oil in a frying pan to 350° F (175° C).

4. Fry each cutlet for 3-4 minutes per side until golden brown and cooked through.

5. Drain on a wire rack or paper towels.

6. Slice into strips and serve with tonkatsu sauce and shredded cabbage.

PORK TENDERLOIN SANDWICH

The pork tenderloin sandwich is unofficial Indiana royalty. Culturally and calorically, the sandwich stands atop diner, pub, and drive-in menus from Evansville to Elkhart.

So, what's different in Carmel? We don't fry crispier tenderloins or bake softer rolls. No secret sauces or seasonings. What makes our version of this deep-fried behemoth of a sandwich taste so good?

The answer, like most of the city's best features, comes down to relationships and community. That sounds pretty lame. This is a recipe book, not a feel-good commercial, I know. Just let me explain.

The process starts just after sunrise in Carmel's Arts & Design District, the eight-block commercial hub connecting Carmel High School to the Monon Trail. Most of Main Street is sleeping. A 2x4 sign, identifying JOE'S BUTCHER SHOP FISH MARKET against the uniform pattern of brick storefronts, hangs above the sidewalk. Joe Lazzara parks, unlocks the front door, and flips on the lights. This is where the sandwich begins.

Joe's Butcher Shop raised the standard of Carmel's food culture. Lazzara started Joe's in 2006 with a simple mission: bring high-quality, locally-sourced meat to the community. Specifically, meat from farms that don't rely on corporate focus groups or million-dollar advertising budgets. Almost immediately, customers noticed the local difference. Restaurants did, too.

Back in Carmel, it's now 9:30 a.m. Lazzara drives to Dooley O'Tooles, a local spot for Indiana comfort food since 1985. The owner, Doug Kemp, walks outside, shakes Lazzara's hand, and inspects the boxes. It's a symbolic step, honestly, because the cargo hasn't changed in years: fresh pork tenderloin.

The first thing I saw at Dooley O'Tooles was the glow of orange neon around the pub's wood-paneled entryway. It was lunchtime on Tuesday, meaning only one thing: Tenderloin Tuesday. A small sign by the door marked the occasion:

TENDERLOIN TUESDAY
Back by Popular Demand

According to Kemp, the kitchen serves up over one hundred tenderloins for the weekly occasion. Three digits of pork cutlet—pounded, breaded, and deep-fried—every single Tuesday. I slid into a corner booth, thinking Tenderloin Tuesday may deserve its own holiday alongside Black Friday and Palm Sunday. Five minutes later, my frisbee-sized sandwich arrived. I strained to search for the plate's white outline behind a blanket of fried pork. The sandwich blotted out the sun.

I've never wrestled or fought jujitsu, but I imagine the opening thirty seconds of a fight—grappling, twisting, feeling out your opponent's defenses—are not unlike the struggle of maneuvering

that first bite of pork tenderloin. The cutlet juts out over the bun, almost cartoonishly so. It's dense, oily, and impossible to pick up like a burger. You just don't have the angle.

The sandwich is ultimately worth the struggle it exacts, though. The tenderloin's exterior holds a generous crunch that gently gives to the fatty pork inside. It's the kind of meal you could really enjoy maybe once or twice a month and then opt for salad the following week. If that's not your thing, if deep-fried brown isn't your color, pork tenderloin may not be for you. That's okay. Tenderloin Tuesday isn't a federal holiday—not yet.

PORK TENDERLOIN SANDWICH

(Makes 4 sandwiches)

INGREDIENTS

○ 1 pound pork tenderloin, cut into 4 equal pieces

○ 1 cup buttermilk

○ 1 teaspoon salt

○ 1/2 teaspoon black pepper

○ 1/2 teaspoon garlic powder

○ 1/2 teaspoon paprika

○ 1 cup all-purpose flour

○ 1 cup crushed saltine crackers or panko breadcrumbs

○ 1 egg, beaten

○ Oil (for frying)

○ 4 sandwich buns

For Serving (Optional)

○ Mayonnaise

○ Mustard

○ Pickles

○ Lettuce

○ Tomato

○ Onion

① Place each pork piece between plastic wrap and pound to about 1/4 -inch thickness.

② In a bowl, mix buttermilk, salt, pepper, garlic powder, and paprika. Add pork and marinate for at least 1 hour (or overnight).

③ Set up a breading station with three shallow dishes: one with flour, one with beaten egg, and one with crushed crackers or panko.

④ Remove pork from buttermilk, letting excess drip off. Dredge in flour, dip in egg, then coat with crackers/panko, pressing to adhere.

⑤ Heat 1/2 inch of vegetable oil in a skillet to 350° F (175° C). Fry each tenderloin for 2-3 minutes per side until golden brown and crispy.

⑥ Drain on a wire rack or paper towels.

⑦ Serve on sandwich buns with desired toppings.

PORK TENDERLOIN SANDWICH

69

BOSCO STICKS

I graduated from Carmel High School almost a decade ago. Forget the sports, and forget the grades. Only one thing can still make me nostalgic: Bosco Sticks.

It's a dish that confounds as much as it comforts. I've never seen it on a restaurant menu. I've never seen it outside a school cafeteria, actually. Bosco Sticks would appear on the menu at random— a Tuesday here, a Friday there—for the five or so years I attended public school in Indiana. The whole thing felt totally classy and European. By the time my grade entered high school, we had been conditioned to drool at the sight of the vaguely Italian packaging. No one questioned the routine or its nutritional value. All we knew was that they tasted great.

I realize now that Bosco Sticks are not sophisticated. They're breadsticks, stuffed with melted string cheese and served with cups of tomato sauce and ranch dressing.

I knew I needed to talk about Camel High School in this cookbook. But my memory of high school was spotty; cafeteria food, even more so. Before I could write about the Sticks, I needed to go back to the source.

Thankfully, I had someone on the inside. My youngest sister, Elsie, had just started high school. She took classes in what Carmel calls the "Freshman Center," an enclosed wing of the school dedicated to first-year students. Her locker, classrooms, and cafeteria were all located within the same block. I briefed her on the plan, glossing over the obvious focus on Bosco Sticks. Two weeks later, I showed up at the Freshman Center, ready for lunch.

Carmel High School is notoriously big. Every graduating class boasts over 1,000 students—mine was well over that number. On any given day, Carmel's three cafeterias hold almost 5,000 students. But, walking through the Freshman Center, the school didn't feel like a lunch party for 5,000. It was clean, compact, and organized.

Elsie guided us to the cafeteria and left to grab seats, leaving me alone in the line of students. The freshmen cafeteria is divided into three sections: the stage, elevated off the floor by a few steps; the seating area, made up of thirty round, eight-seat lunch tables; and the kitchen—three U-shaped industrial bays mixing and serving lunch for the students who buy lunch at school.

I reached the front of the line, grabbed a tray, and surveyed my options. Breaded chicken sandwiches wrapped in thin, shiny foil. Small, clear, to-go containers of Caesar salad. An array of corn, celery, and cherry tomatoes. And then, near the end of the buffet spread, Bosco Sticks.

I'm convinced high school cafeterias pump in their own type of electricity. A palpable, nervous electricity, like you're on live television for the first time and no one, not even the camera guy, can guarantee what's going to happen next, and people are watching and perceiving you in a way that's almost entirely not up to you. It doesn't help when you're a twenty-four-year-old wading through a sea of fourteen-year-olds, guarding a plastic tray of breadsticks. Elsie, mercifully, waved me down.

I could feel the sticks still warm in their paper bag. Elsie's friends seemed confused. "You're just here to eat those?"

"Yeah," I said, trying to sound casual while explaining the cookbook, my trip to Kawachinagano, and the upcoming sister city anniversary. They nodded politely. As far as lunch conversation goes, I was no competition for Olivia Rodrigo or the upcoming WNBA Draft. Turning back to my tray, I pulled out a Bosco Stick and took a bite.

Two thoughts came to mind:
1. Wow, this really is just a breadstick, a little undercooked, stuffed with rubbery cheese. The whole thing was probably frozen solid twenty-four hours earlier.
2. Damn. Nostalgia sucks.

Bosco Sticks are not a metaphor for youth, and this chapter is not a therapy session. But I am constantly surprised that meals—and memories of meals—are just as much products of time, place, and emotion as they are flavor. My quest to reclaim a piece of high school was hopeless because those Bosco Sticks are still in 2017, and there's no secret exit off the Freshman Center that leads back there. And that's a good thing. We can't look back too often, even for the Sticks.

BOSCO STICKS

INGREDIENTS

○ 2 1/4 teaspoons (1 packet) active dry yeast

○ 3/4 cup warm water (about 110° F)flour for gluten-free)

○ 1 teaspoon sugar

○ 2 cups all-purpose flour

○ 1 teaspoon salt

○ 1 tablespoon olive oil

○ 8 string cheese sticks (mozzarella)

○ 2 tablespoons butter, melted

○ 1/2 teaspoon garlic powder

○ 1/2 teaspoon Italian seasoning

○ 1/4 cup grated Parmesan cheese

INSTRUCTIONS

1. Dissolve yeast and sugar in warm water and let sit for 5-10 minutes until foamy.

2. In a large bowl, combine flour and salt. Add yeast mixture and olive oil, then knead for about 5 minutes until smooth. Cover and let rise for 1 hour, or until doubled in size.

3. Preheat oven to 375° F. Divide dough into 8 pieces and flatten each into a rectangle. Place a string cheese stick in the center and wrap dough around it, pinching the edges to seal. Arrange on a parchment-lined baking sheet.

4. Bake for 12-15 minutes, or until golden brown. Brush with melted butter and sprinkle with garlic powder, Italian seasoning, and Parmesan cheese. Serve warm with marinara sauce for dipping.

YAKISOBA PAN

The walk to Seikyo Gakuen is only a "walk" in the figurative sense of the word. In truth, it's a hike. The school sits atop a mountain near Kawachinagano Central Station, with hundreds of stairs carving an imposing path through trees and morning sunlight all the way to Seikyo's sprawling campus. At Carmel High School, we have "The Trail," a quarter-mile uphill slope connecting the stadium parking lot to the school's north entrance. The hike to Seikyo Gakuen requires a different vocabulary altogether. It's not a journey I'd wish on anyone running late to first period.

Seikyo Gakuen is a long-standing pillar of the Carmel-Kawachinagano relationship. The ties between Seikyo and Carmel High School actually predate Carmel's relationship with Kawachinagano. The two schools formed a formal agreement in March 1991, three years before the cities signed an official sister city agreement. Seikyo-Carmel exchange dates all the way back to 1987.

At the top of the stairs, I met Morino-san, the school's longtime English teacher and now-principal. Morino-san wore a grey suit, frameless glasses, and a white disposable mask. He spoke clear, quiet English with the ease of someone who had been teaching the language professionally for decades. For over thirty years, Morino-san organized Seikyo's student delegations to Carmel. It started to feel like Seikyo was not just a pillar of Kawachinagano's relationship with Carmel but its core.

Seikyo students, donning the school's signature dark uniforms, nodded respectfully as Morino-san and I passed through the hallway. In Japan, most secondary school students wear uniforms—ensembles of sweaters, skirts, high socks, blazers, and bow ties. Seikyo is no different. Boys wear dark navy blazers, white button-downs, and striped emerald ties. Girls wear blazers, dark skirts, and bow ties of the same emerald shade. More casual students ditch their blazers, perhaps with a hint of rebellion, for a V-neck cardigan (tie present, of course). I noticed how long my hair looked in comparison to the Seikyo boys' hair. Short, neat hair was part of the dress code, it seemed. I asked Morino-san about my shaggy cut. "Don't worry, we'd fix it," he said.

We left the teacher's lounge and slipped into the stream of students headed to the cafeteria. Lunch was ready.

Something in the corner of the cafeteria, near the outdoor patio, caught my eye. It was roughly the size and shape of a vending machine, with bright, glowing buttons across its front. I watched a student walk up to the machine, insert a few coins, and press a button glowing on the display. Almost instantly, the machine shot out a small paper ticket. She grabbed the ticket, joined another line near the kitchen, and handed it to the cook behind the counter. The cook turned back to his brigade and re-emerged seconds later with a steaming bowl of soba noodles. The school's kitchen did it all. If the vending machine printed it, the kitchen could make it.

I punched out a curry rice ticket, handed it to the cook, and headed outside to join Morino-san on the patio. As I walked past the pastry shelf, I noticed a curious, plastic-wrapped bun. It vaguely resembled a hot dog bun, with the same horizontal cut down the middle. But instead of a beef dog, the bun encased a handful of yakisoba noodles. It was jarring—the kind of meal you'd dream up in college at 3 a.m. In Japan, it's known as yakisoba-pan. I'd call it carbs-on-carbs.

The noodle-bun sandwich has a strong presence in Japan, Morino-san assured me. It's a cheap, reliable snack to get through math class or a filling lunch when normal options sour. I picked one out, unwrapped the plastic foil, and took a bite. The yakisoba-pan

It's a dense, chaotic partnership of textures and starches.

actually tasted good once I accepted this was no hot dog. The fried noodles soaked into the surrounding bun, forging a dense, chaotic partnership of textures and starches. Across the table, Morino-san seemed to approve. And, I realized, all my carb-loading would pay off. I still needed to hike down the mountain after school.

YAKISOBA PAN

(Makes 4 sandwiches)

INGREDIENTS

○ 4 hot dog buns
○ 2 packs (about 6 oz each) yakisoba noodles
○ 1/2 cup thinly sliced cabbage
○ 1/2 small onion, thinly sliced
○ 1/2 small carrot, sliced into matchsticks
○ 1/2 bell pepper, thinly sliced (optional)
○ 1/2 cup thinly sliced pork belly or chicken (optional)
○ 1 tablespoon vegetable oil
○ 2 tablespoons yakisoba sauce
○ 1 teaspoon soy sauce
○ 1/2 teaspoon sesame oil (optional)

For Topping

○ Pickled ginger
○ Mayo (optional)
○ Toasted sesame seeds

① Heat vegetable oil in a pan over medium-high heat.

② Add pork or chicken (if using) and cook until browned. Add onions, carrots, and bell pepper, stir-frying for 1-2 minutes.

③ Add cabbage and yakisoba noodles, breaking up the noodles as they soften. Pour in yakisoba sauce, soy sauce, and sesame oil. Stir-fry until evenly coated and heated through.

④ Lightly toast the hot dog buns if desired.

⑤ Fill each bun with a generous amount of yakiso-ba. Top with pickled ginger and a drizzle of mayo if desired.

⑥ Serve warm and enjoy.

WALKING TACO

Imagine a taco. There's ground meat, cheese, lettuce, diced tomatoes, and maybe some sour cream or salsa. And, of course, a tortilla shell. Now imagine trying to eat that taco while you're running late to a meeting, rushing down the sidewalk, meat and sour cream dripping everywhere as you try to cradle the shell. It's not pretty.

The walking taco is Indiana's spill-free solution—equal parts inspiration and improvisation. We skip the taco shell altogether. All the normal fillings are still there, but instead of the shell, we scoop everything into a snack-size bag of salty corn chips. Shake it up and enjoy—sitting, standing, or walking.

The concept sounds wrong, deeply weird, and perhaps even insensitive to the wider taco community. But there's a fondness in Carmel for this Frankenstein-like alternative. I've seen walking tacos everywhere, from the school cafeteria to the weekend farmers market. I didn't fully understand the appeal, however, until I tried one for myself at Carmel's International Arts Festival.

The setting seemed like the perfect place for a stress-test: thousands of visitors walking booth-to-booth, up and down Main Street. I put in my order. One taco—walking, please—with extra salsa and no sour cream. The vendor ladled everything into a bag of Fritos, shook it up, and handed it to me with a plastic fork and a nod.

You don't have to love the idea. You don't even have to like it. All that I ask is that you consider its utility and respect its indulgence. Eyes closed, it's 80 percent taco—it even has a crunch. And, as I navigated the festival, tacos in hand, dodging wood carvings, sculptures, and eager tourists alike, I didn't miss that other 20 percent.

WALKING TACO

(Makes 6 servings)

INGREDIENTS

- 1 lb ground beef (or turkey)
- 1 packet taco seasoning
- 1/2 cup water
- 6 snack-sized bags of Fritos (or other chip)
- 1 cup shredded cheddar cheese
- 1 cup shredded lettuce
- 1/2 cup diced tomatoes
- 1/2 cup sour cream

INSTRUCTIONS

1. Cook ground beef in a skillet over medium heat. Drain excess grease.
2. Add taco seasoning and water, then simmer for 5 minutes until thickened.
3. Carefully cut open the side of each chip bag.
4. Spoon taco meat into each bag, then add cheese, lettuce, tomatoes, and other toppings as desired.
5. Mix everything up with a fork and enjoy straight from the bag.

UDON

The world of Japanese noodles is pretty much endless. With each family comes a genus, and with that, new variations of taste, size, and technique. One quickly learns to draw broad associations.

You have soba, the thin buckwheat noodles served cold with soy sauce or hot in a clear broth. It's heart-healthy, high in protein and fiber, and makes for an easy, on-the-go lunch. Another staple, ramen, is instantly brandable and unquestionably delicious, with hundreds of broths, add-ins, and seasonings.

Where does that leave udon? The thick, chewy noodle isn't hearty like soba or flashy like ramen.

I'd argue that udon is the most reliable noodle in Japan. With a few exceptions, like the indulgent curry udon (*kare udon*), it does not change. In this sense, it's earned the distinction of timeless comfort food. Good udon is fresh, firm, and doesn't stray from its fundamental flavors in the same way ramen seems to flaunt its own. A bowl of udon, just wheat noodles and dashi broth, is so simple that most recipe lists could fit on a postage stamp.

Kawachinagano may just have the best udon in all of Osaka Prefecture. A few years ago, Miyoshiya moved into downtown Kawachinagano. Miyoshiya's owner, Hiro-san, is nearly as famous as his udon. Before moving to Kawachinagano, he opened noodle shops from Namba to Sakai City and almost launched at least one freezer-aisle udon brand.

Miyoshiya sits right along a scenic bend in the Kōya Kaido trail, the road cutting straight through town and stretching to Mount Kōya in Wakayama Prefecture. If it all sounds slightly pilgrimage-like, that's because it is. The Kōya Kaido links over eighty-eight religious sites from Kyoto to Osaka to Mount Kōya.

Miyoshiya's interior is distinctly homey, with faded wooden tables, warm lights, and dangling frames lining the perimeter of the dining room. It naturally amplified the grandparent charm of Hiro-san and his wife, Norie-san. Norie-san greeted me as I slid open the wooden door and removed my shoes. She wore a tan apron, wide-frame wire glasses, and a black beret tilted over her long, gray hair.

Her smile covered her whole face when she laughed. Hiro-san appeared from the kitchen moments later with a deep, echoing laugh. "I'm so happy!" he exclaimed—the first of many times that afternoon. His enthusiasm is part of the place's charm, so much so that a sketch of his grin—mouth wide, eyes shut behind his tiny, round-rimmed glasses, beard and mustache trimmed—is the shop's official logo.

Hiro-san's udon class was a full-body workout. I rocked back and forth, first kneading the dough, then pounding it into thin, flat sheets. When that still wasn't thin enough, we wrapped the sheets in plastic and took turns jumping on them.

Hiro-san's step-by-step instructions blurred into impromptu life coaching, with questions (what do you want in life?), advice (you must be present in the little moments), and many signature declarations of happiness. Then he gathered our noodles and left for the kitchen, returning just moments later with fresh, steaming bowls of udon.

The steaming noodles glistened as my bowl hit the table. A smaller bowl full of dark brown broth sat nearby on the table. I held my chopsticks gingerly, maneuvering the udon out of its bowl, down into the broth, and quickly up into my mouth. Hiro-san's udon was a harmony of taste and texture. I finished my bowl and quickly started on another. To borrow a phrase from Hiro-san, I was happy.

Udon is the most
reliable noodle in Japan.

UDON

(Makes about 4 servings)

INGREDIENTS

- ○ 2 cups (250g) all-purpose flour
- ○ 1/2 cup (120ml) warm water
- ○ 1/2 teaspoon salt

INSTRUCTIONS

① In a small bowl, dissolve salt in warm water.

② In a large mixing bowl, add flour and gradually pour in the saltwater, mixing until a rough dough forms.

③ Knead the dough for about 10 minutes until it becomes smooth and elastic.

④ Wrap in plastic wrap and let rest at room temperature for 1-2 hours.

⑤ Roll out the dough on a lightly floured surface to about 1/8 inch thick.

⑥ Fold the dough gently and slice into 1/4-inch wide strips.

⑦ Dust the noodles with flour to prevent sticking.

⑧ Bring a large pot of water to a boil and cook noodles for 10-12 minutes until chewy but tender.

⑨ Drain, rinse with cold water, and serve.

TEMAKI SUSHI

Sushi is not the type of food that requires an introduction, so I won't try to introduce it. There are plenty of travel guides, to-do lists, and itineraries that have done that for decades. Sushi is iconic; it's practically synonymous with Japan itself. I will state the obvious, though, which is that "sushi" does not imply the same thing everywhere. To say Nobu and Kroger both make sushi is true, but only in a passing way. Roger Federer and I both play tennis, technically.

Why is this important? Only because I didn't know how sushi really tasted until I got to Kawachinagano. I was leaving the train station at lunchtime and passed a winding line of businessmen queuing outside of a supply closet. They'd wait, silently scrolling their phones, step inside, and exit out a side door thirty seconds later with a white shopping bag. I studied the loop for ten minutes before deferring to the only time-tested rule I have for discovering great food: When you see a line, get in it.

That was the first place I ate sushi in Japan. Not in the supply closet, which turned out to be a tiny, to-go sushi spot, but at the bus stop outside Kawachinagano Station. I caught the signal at the front of the shop's queue—a universal "you're up" hand-gesture instead of formal Japanese—and stepped up to the register. Everything looked good. I pointed once, nodded twice, and left with a sample platter.

My little 700-yen ($4.50) box was the best sushi I'd ever had. I remember every bite. I think people getting on and off the bus were staring. Who cares?

The history of sushi follows the story of its main ingredients: rice and fish. Originally, the combo was a matter of practicality. Fresh fish wrapped in fermented rice could keep for up to a year in the right conditions. This practice was called *narezushi* and dates to China in the fourth century BC.

Narezushi emerged in Japan several centuries later. Fish was always a natural fit in the country's ocean-dependent diet, and any process that could extend its longevity was happily embraced. However, by the Muromachi period (1336–1573), *narezushi* proved too time-consuming. A style of sushi called *namanare-zushi*, which only required partial fermentation, began to catch on. And, unlike its Chinese predecessor, this new style didn't discard any ingredients. The fermented rice and fish were eaten together.

Styles like *narezushi* and *namanare-zushi* developed into what we call sushi today. There's sashimi, thin-sliced raw fish; nigiri sushi, a cut of raw fish atop a bed of rice; and maki sushi, a rice and nori seaweed roll with fish inside. These are usually what non-Japanese think of when they think of sushi. There are countless others, like Osaka-style oshizushi. But back in Kawachinagano, I had my eye on a different type of sushi altogether: conveyor-belt.

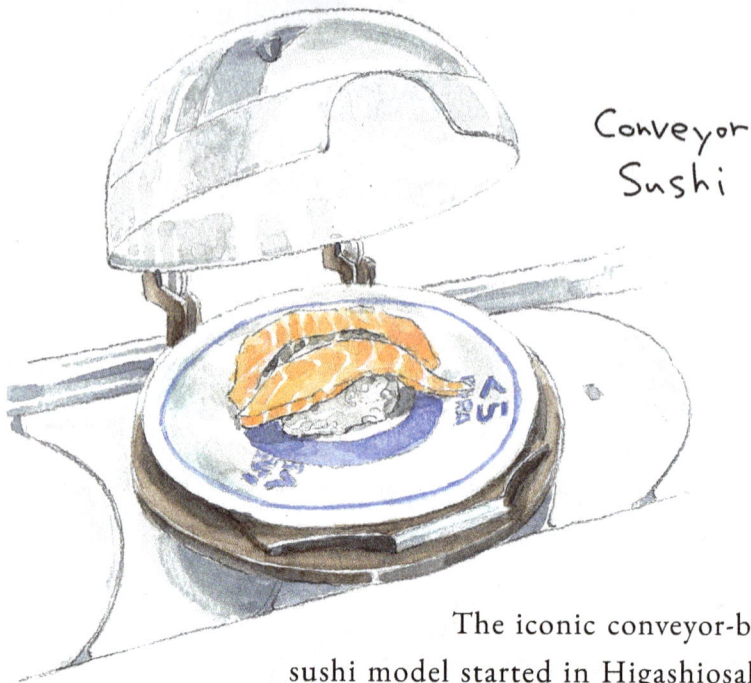

Conveyor Sushi

The iconic conveyor-belt sushi model started in Higashiosaka, Osaka, about forty minutes from Kawachinagano. The inventor, restaurant owner Yoshiaki Shiraishi, apparently found his inspiration while watching the assembly line at a beer factory. Soon after Shiraishi's success, conveyor-style sushi shops spread throughout Japan. Now, almost every city in Japan boasts a belt. Kawachinagano is no different.

On a cold December afternoon, I hopped out of Yamamoto-san's car and met the KIFA staff in front of Kurazushi Harachoten, Kawachinagano's conveyor-belt sushi shop. The restaurant sits right off National Route 170, a two-lane highway connecting eastern Osaka through the countryside. The wider neighborhood is contoured by a perfect triangle of City Hall, McDonalds, and Second Street thrift shop—all within a three-block radius. I knew the area well.

The six of us (me, Harumi-san, Hiroko-san, Yamamoto-san, Megumi-san, and Iisaka-sensei) settled into a booth along the perimeter of the conveyor belt. Yamamoto-san and I sat furthest inside the booth, right next to the sushi belt. He explained that this spot carried a unique responsibility. We were the first line of defense, the advanced team, in charge of selecting sushi from the belt for our table.

We began eyeing the different plates as they passed our view. Megumi-san scanned a QR code and pulled up a form to order everything from tuna sashimi to french fries. This explained the shop's dual-belt system: the bottom belt was a local uptown train—stopping at every station, slow, reliable. If you missed a plate you'd see the next one in a couple minutes. The top belt ran express, so all you heard was a small warning beep, and a plate of shrimp tempura would zip past you. Megumi-san explained that the QR codes were synced with the express belt, and whatever we ordered would stop right at our table. My attempts to capture the process on video failed. There was about 1.85 seconds between the warning beep and a blur of bright sushi flying to its destination. It was an ingenuous setup. Any operation that can sling seared salmon at Mach 1 has my immediate attention.

Temaki
Zushi

I tried temaki sushi for the first time that day. I saw the photo while scrolling through the menu on Megumi-san's phone—a crepe-like pocket of salmon wrapped in a seaweed cone. I surveyed the group. *Temaki, hmm, okay, yes, let's get three.* A few minutes later, we heard the beep, looked over, and there they were.

To me, temaki is great because it's forgiving. Its quality is not overly determined by precision or aesthetics. Flavor is key. So is practicality. Because of its unique, hand-rolled shape, the sushi holds its contents—fish, rice, green onions, avocado—together in a dense, cone-shaped jumble. It's easy to pick up and eat. It's easy to make and serve, too, even without a conveyor belt.

TEMAKI SUSHI

(Makes 4 rolls)

INGREDIENTS

- 1 cup sushi rice, cooked
- 2 tablespoons rice vinegar
- 1 teaspoon sugar
- 1/2 teaspoon salt
- 4 sheets nori (seaweed), cut in half
- 4 ounces fresh raw salmon, sliced into strips
- 1/4 cup cucumber, sliced into matchsticks
- 1/4 cup avocado, sliced

INSTRUCTIONS

1. In a small bowl, mix rice vinegar, sugar, and salt, then fold into warm sushi rice. Let cool to room temperature.

2. Place a seaweed sheet on a dry surface (shiny side down).

3. Scoop about 2 tablespoons of sushi rice onto the left side of the nori, spreading it lightly.

4. Place salmon, cucumber, and avocado diagonally across the rice.

5. Fold the bottom left corner over the filling and roll into a cone shape. Use water to seal the edges if needed.

6. Repeat with remaining ingredients.

7. Serve with soy sauce, wasabi, and pickled ginger.

MATCHA

The tea ceremony at Kongō-ji Temple started with a welcome. There were twelve of us, mostly staff from KIFA and City Hall. We took off our shoes, ducked through the low doorway, and bowed to Sowa-san, our gray-haired host sitting across the tatami-mat interior. I shuffled to a low stool near the perimeter. The more dexterous guests opted for a spot directly on the mat, folding their legs beneath themselves in a kneeling posture. One by one, Sowa-san offered each of us a dessert made from sweet bean paste. "This is *wagashi*," she whispered to me, breaking the room's silence.

She returned to her table and began warming the *chagama*, a traditional cast iron pot for boiling tea water. Her kimono betrayed no excess movement. We sat in a half circle, watching steam start to rise off the water. No one spoke.

Sowa-san gathered a spoonful of matcha and placed it into a small ceramic bowl. She added three ladles of boiling water, lifted a bamboo whisk, and, bracing the side of the bowl with her left hand, began flicking the matcha around with her right wrist. The tea started to foam. Our host carried the first bowl to my seat, knelt, and presented it forward with both hands. My turn to continue the choreography.

In tea ceremonies, the host always serves with the bowl's front, usually the most ornate side, facing the recipient. Like so many other details throughout the ceremony, this movement is all about respect. The host respects her guest by presenting the bowl's best side. The guest—in this case, me—bows to thank the host and receives the tea with both hands: left on the bottom and right at the bowl's side.

I rotated the bowl clockwise until the front was no longer facing me. With this one gesture, I signaled admiration for the design and, more importantly, my respect for the host by not drinking from the front of the bowl.

I barely remember my first sip of matcha. I was too focused on receiving the bowl, turning it at least ninety degrees, and raising it properly to my lips. The second sip, however, was impossible to forget. This wasn't matcha in its commercialized Frappuccino form. This was strong, slightly bitter, and perfectly smooth. I finished my bowl with a third sip, bowed once more, and passed it back to our host. The dance continued.

DINNER

BUTTERMILK RANCH

Community spaces are hard to define. There's something organic about them, a feeling that transcends easy classification. The word "belonging" strikes a partial definition, but not belonging in the exclusive, country club sense. More like in the way you can belong to a sports team or a friend group. Local restaurants and libraries fit that definition. And Woodys Library Restaurant—both a library and restaurant—certainly fits as well.

Before the bi-level, brick-exterior house was a neighborhood staple, it was Carmel's local library. In 1913, the Carnegie Corporation (as in Andrew Carnegie, the American billionaire) provided an $11,000 grant to build the city's first public library. The library opened in 1914 and stood until 1972, when the city converted it into a courthouse. When Kevin Ryder opened Woodys in 1998, there was almost no need to remodel—the place already felt like part of the community.

The first night Ryder opened his doors—just the downstairs bar, not even the restaurant—over 160 people showed up.

Ryder and his wife, Richelle, run the restaurant on two principles: quality and variety. "Never be known for a favorite thing on your menu," Ryder told me, sitting up against the counter at Woodys' bar. He speaks about the business with a technical, accountant-like sureness, so much so that I knew he had been a consultant without asking. (Like a good interviewer, I did. He was.) Richelle runs the back of house as the executive chef. To their credit, almost every customer I quizzed claimed a different favorite on the menu.

So, in a sense, I don't feel too bad about allowing my preferences to sway this chapter's recipe. Deciphering an objective ultimate dish from Woodys' menu would require a level of community polling I'm not qualified to conduct. Instead, I'll just tell you that my favorite is the buttermilk ranch.

This condiment is the unsung hero of Woodys' menu. It gets no stand-alone praise, no opportunity for a solo feature. But once you know where to look, you see it all over the menu. It comes with the turkey cobb, the boneless wings, and, of course, the chicken tenders. I've seen customers put it on salads. I've seen it dunked like a sauce. I wouldn't be surprised to see it eaten with a spoon.

BUTTERMILK RANCH

(Makes about 1½ cups)

INGREDIENTS

- 1/2 cup mayonnaise
- 1/2 cup sour cream
- 1/2 cup buttermilk
- 1 teaspoon lemon juice
- 1 clove garlic, minced
- 1/2 teaspoon onion powder
- 1 teaspoon dill, finely chopped
- 2 teaspoon parsley, finely chopped
- 1 teaspoon chives, finely chopped
- 1/2 teaspoon salt
- 1/4 teaspoon black pepper

INSTRUCTIONS

1. In a medium bowl, whisk together the mayonnaise, sour cream, and buttermilk until smooth.

2. Stir in the lemon juice.

3. Add the garlic, onion powder, dill, parsley, chives, salt, and pepper. Whisk until fully combined.

4. Cover and refrigerate for at least 30 minutes (or up to 24 hours) to let the flavors meld.

5. Taste and adjust seasoning if needed. If too thick, add a splash more buttermilk.

TAKOYAKI

Four days before arriving in Kawachinagano, I got a cryptic email.

> I am a staff member of Kawachinagano City Hall. Terumichi Higashi. Please contact me if you don't mind.

My thumb hovered over the screen. Was it spam? Was it a test? I weighed my response.

"Hi Higashi-san," I wrote back. "Looking forward to arriving in your beautiful city. Please let me know what information you need. For reference, my flight will arrive at Itami Airport at 8:30 p.m. local time on October 1."

> Ok. See you then.

A single sentence. Something, it seemed, was about to go down at Itami Airport.

Seventy-two hours later, I emerged through the baggage claim at Itami Airport. My eyes darted around the perimeter. The hall was empty except for one or two employees corralling a chain of stray luggage carts. Across the hall, the baggage carousel shot on with a series of beeps, spitting dark cases of luggage onto the conveyor belt.

I grabbed my bags and turned to leave, still unsure of what—or whom—to expect outside. A short, well-dressed man standing near the exit sign caught my attention. I recognized his hat's yellow-red logo: CARMEL FIRE DEPARTMENT.

He smiled. It was Terumichi Higashi, my first friend in Kawachi-nagano.

"I recognized you from your appearance," he relayed through the small translation gadget he always kept with him. It was still the first week of October, and Japan hadn't yet lifted its travel restrictions on foreign tourists. Appearance, I thought, was a diplomatic way of saying I was the only white guy in Arrivals after 11:00 p.m. on a Saturday night.

As we exchanged business cards, he suddenly threw up his hand, as if signaling me to wait, and dug into his brown leather shoulder bag. He retrieved five pieces of paper, all held together with tape like a chain. On each page, printed in enormous size 750 font, was a single letter. One page at a time, Higashi-san unfurled an E-T-H-A-N banner above his head.

I saw Higashi-san several more times throughout October. He joined my project updates at Kawachinagano City Hall, always sitting silently at the back of the room. Occasionally, we met for lunch at the tiny cafe near his office.

"First month, focus on specific foods. Month two and month

three, broader themes of food culture." Higashi-san's eyes were wide, his face completely serious. He stretched across the table, pushing his electronic Japanese-to-English translator right up to my face. I nodded faintly, distracted by the plates of curry rice in front of us. Outside the window, a late-October breeze brushed around City Hall, pushing dark red leaves around the pavilion.

"I would like to show you my elementary school," Higashi-san continued. "Monday, they will host the traditional Sports Day." Finally, I thought, some action. I imagined hundreds of screaming fans, flushed with Kawachinagano pride, stomping up and down on gymnasium seats. We shook hands. Higashi-san, as always, went to pay for lunch. I started to prepare a mental list of tailgate snacks.

Early Monday morning, Higashi-san's Toyota pulled up to the Tsunamoto's house in Ichicho. Students in sleek black uniforms flowed around the car on bicycles. Higashi-san, donning his CAR-MEL FIRE DEPARTMENT cap, held up a pre-typed message on his translator as I opened the passenger door. "Good morning. We will very much enjoy today."

We left Ichicho, winding deeper into the Osaka countryside on our way to Amami Primary School. "Amami," Higashi-san said as we paused at a red light, "is a special place." He wasn't kidding. The school's total enrollment last year—spanning first through sixth grade—was just sixty-three students. In Japanese, it's classified as a *shōkibo tokunin-kō*, or "small-scale special school," meaning students from anywhere in Kawachinagano can qualify to attend.

Outside my window, Kawachinagano's palette of green, red, and yellow foliage started to blend together. After years of biking this route as a student, Higashi-san seemed to anticipate every turn. He suddenly veered left, revealing a small cluster of school buildings in the distance. All of Amami's facilities, including an outdoor swimming pool and small athletic field, tuck into the side of a sloping hill. We pulled to a stop, parked, and joined the stream of parents descending toward the school—a tiny jewel embedded in the countryside.

The dusty athletic field was already packed with students wearing their uniforms: gym sneakers, white socks, and white T-shirts tucked into dark blue shorts. There were two distinct teams, each with its own chin-strapped baseball cap. White for one team, red for the other.

I turned to Higashi-san. "When does the match start?" I asked, implying my hope we'd be watching soccer or maybe rugby. He looked up from the program and shook his head. "No match," he said. "Tug-of-war in ten minutes."

Slowly, white hats and red hats began lining up near the south entrance of the track. An old speaker sputtered to life and filled the grounds with a marching tune. After a lap around the track, the two teams lined up facing each other, separated by eight PVC-like poles painted half red and half white. Younger students cheered expectantly from the far end of the track. Above them, a rusty scoreboard hung from the jungle gym. Red, 47. White, 85. We started pulling for the red hats.

All around the country, schoolchildren were running, jumping, and cheering in similarly adorable fashion. In Japan, the second Monday of October is a public holiday: Sports Day (*Supōtsu No Hi*). Most schools throughout Japan, and even some businesses, host events to commemorate the 1964 Tokyo Olympics, complete with track relays, ball tosses, and, in Amami's local interpretation, tug-of-war.

My favorite tradition occurred after the final race of the day. Both teams, the white hats having staved off a comeback, left the track and found their families in the shade. It was time to eat. We waded into the picnic, stepping over blankets and strollers as we surveyed each family's spread.

It was the tailgate equivalent of an art gallery. Each lunch box (bentō) contained a unique configuration of rice dumplings (onigiri), pickled vegetables (tsukemono), and rolled omelets (tamagoyaki). Higashi-san walked by each family and introduced our visit. The preparation for most family-sized spreads, we learned, started at dawn.

I realize picnic-style bentō wasn't a feature of the 1964 Games in Tokyo, but Amami Primary makes a strong case for its inclusion. I'd be first in line to advocate its future Olympic inclusion. Or second—right behind Higashi-san.

After meeting Amami's principal—the same lean, middle-aged man who had earlier anchored a very convincing 400-meter relay—Higashi-san and I climbed back into the Toyota. Higashi-san couldn't hide his smile. His former classmates had spotted him the minute we arrived at the track. As much as Sports Day was a student holiday, it was also an opportunity for parents, alumni, and former teachers to reconnect. Given the school's size, I had met almost half of Higashi-san's graduating class. Amami was special.

We sped off, watching the buildings fade as we drove deeper into the countryside. Higashi-san flipped on his headlights as the road turned into a narrow dirt driveway. "I want to show you Kawachi-nagano farmer food," he said.

I stepped through the entryway of Higashi-san's family home, slipped off my shoes, and found my seat in the adjacent hosting room. Higashi-san had invited two friends from City Hall to join us for dinner. The four of us exchanged business cards around a typical short-legged tea table, the *chabudai*. "Dinner is ready," Higashi-san announced a few minutes later.

We walked through the hallway into a small, tiled kitchen. Two chairs had been added to a round wooden table in the corner of the room. Higashi-san's mother darted around the kitchen at full speed, slowing only momentarily to bow in our direction. She sliced open a full head of lettuce, raising her elbow high over the counter to push through the knife. Before I noticed, our dinner table disappeared under a pile of bowls, sauces, and spices.

This was takoyaki. One of those sloppy, bizarre, delicious foods that confirms Osaka's reputation as the kitchen of Japan.

Tako means octopus, and *yaki* comes from the verb *yaku*, "to grill." I watched Higashi-san rouse this etymology live at the table with long, wooden chopsticks in hand. He turned on a circular cast-iron griddle, specially designed with twelve perfect, golf ball-sized divots, and swiftly greased each hole with a swipe of oil. He poured in the flour batter, filling each hole until it was flush with the surface of the griddle. His friends added the filling: diced octopus (the *tako*), corn, and dried shrimp. Then, more batter—this time to submerge the filling. Higashi-san effortlessly turned each dough ball in its place, allowing the takoyaki to cook evenly. I tried the flipping motion myself, but I quickly punctured the raw dough and spilled corn across the griddle. Eating was more my thing, anyway.

I learned that homemade takoyaki is best made in waves. After one round comes off the griddle, the next quickly fills its place. Eating is constant, highly encouraged, and usually accompanied by several cold beers.

Things were no different at Higashi-san's table. All of us had a role to play in the production. I was eventually promoted to *tako* specialist, a role that involved placing bits of octopus into each batter-filled mold as it cooked. The four of us formed a factory line, devouring the fresh takoyaki balls almost as quickly as we poured on new ones.

"Real Osaka food," Higashi-san murmured as he worked the chopsticks. He was smiling, content with the day's events. All I could do was nod in agreement, but I knew he understood. Food was our common language.

TAKOYAKI

(Makes about 24 pieces)

INGREDIENTS

○ 1 cup (120g) all-purpose flour
○ 1 1/4 cups (300ml) dashi stock (or water with a dash of soy sauce)
○ 1 egg
○ 1/2 teaspoon soy sauce
○ 1/2 teaspoon baking powder
○ 1/2 cup cooked octopus, diced
○ 1/4 cup green onions, chopped
○ 2 tablespoons pickled ginger, minced (optional)
○ vegetable oil (for greasing the pan)

INSTRUCTIONS

① In a bowl, whisk together flour, dashi, egg, soy sauce, and baking powder until smooth.

② Preheat takoyaki pan and brush with oil.

③ Pour batter into the pan, filling each mold nearly to the top.

④ Add octopus, green onions, tempura scraps, and pickled ginger into each mold.

⑤ Let cook for 1-2 minutes, then use skewers or chopsticks to rotate each ball, turning them gradually as they cook.

⑥ Continue rotating until golden brown and crispy on all sides (about 5 minutes).

⑦ Serve hot with takoyaki sauce, mayonnaise, and bonito flakes.

HOT DOGS

For most people, Friday nights are a time to relax, maybe watch a movie, and get ready for the weekend. But in Carmel, at least from August to October, Friday nights have another significance: high school football.

The Carmel Greyhounds' homecoming game was scheduled for the night before my flight to Kawachinagano. I wasn't ready to leave Carmel—I wasn't even fully packed—but I knew I couldn't miss the game. Kickoff was at 7:00 p.m., so I guessed tailgating would start up around 5:30 p.m. That was the extent of my journalistic plan: show up, walk around, and hopefully solicit a hotdog or two.

The anatomy of a tailgate is worth explaining in more detail here. There is usually a car (Carmel High School's parking lot is tailgate HQ), an overhead tent or two, and a few collapsible camping chairs. That's the basic skeleton. Then there's the food: coolers of hamburgers and hot dogs, a tabletop spread of chips and desserts, and (maybe) a vegetable tray. Alcohol is often present, but since the tailgates here occur on high school property, drinking is prohibited. Food is the real nucleus of a good tailgate. And the grill is king.

Maybe that's why my instinct as I neared the football stadium that evening was to follow the smell of barbeque. Kickoff was an hour away, and the parking lot had already converted into a sprawling field of trucks, RVs, and tents. Parents stood in conversation circles of blue and gold. Children ran from tailgate to tailgate, throwing footballs or playing tag, or both. The sun covered the asphalt in an early evening glow.

It was then, admiring the homecoming landscape, that I spotted Perfect Tailgate Dad (PDT for short). Dads throughout Indiana maintain a faint telepathic connection with the nearest barbeque grill. It's a source of strength, an extension of their powers. And PTD was no exception: New Balance sneakers, old-school sunglasses, and a Carmel Greyhounds short sleeve tucked into crisp blue jeans. Undoubtedly his Friday night best.

Food is the nucleus of a good tailgate. And the grill is king.

I walked up to PTD and introduced myself with an all-determining handshake. John (that's PTD's name) introduced himself as the dad appointed to supervise the grill for the cheerleading team's parents/friends/family tailgate. The homecoming game was not, it became obvious, John's first tailgate. He answered my questions casually, but his attention never strayed from the grill. Hotdogs on the left, burgers on the right, and a small pantry of condiments—onion flakes, salt, pepper, and Worcestershire sauce—off to both sides.

Tailgates are about bringing people together, John confirmed, reaching for his tongs. Why else would anyone go through so much effort? His words hit at a deeper truth about food in Carmel. So many of our traditions, including birthdays, holidays, and, dare I say, tailgates, center around food. And not only *what we eat*, but *with whom*. Traditions give us new ways to eat together.

PTD, in a very neighborly, Midwestern way, implied the end of our chat by offering me a hot dog. It was the perfect final evening in Carmel. The Greyhounds won 21-14, I got my hot dog, and most importantly, I finally understood the beauty of a Friday night tailgate.

HOT DOG BUN

(Makes 8 buns)

INGREDIENTS

○ 3/4 cup (180ml) warm milk
○ 2 1/4 teaspoons (1 packet) active dry yeast
○ 2 tablespoons sugar
○ 3 cups (375g) all-purpose flour
○ 1 teaspoon salt
○ 2 tablespoons unsalted butter, softened
○ 1 egg

INSTRUCTIONS

1. In a small bowl, mix warm milk, yeast, and sugar. Let sit for 5-10 minutes until foamy.
2. In a large bowl, combine flour and salt. Add yeast mixture, butter, and egg. Mix until a dough forms.
3. Knead for about 8 minutes until smooth and elastic.
4. Place dough in a greased bowl, cover, and let rise in a warm place for 1-1½ hours.
5. Divide the finished dough into 8 equal pieces. Shape each piece into a log, about 6 inches long.
6. Preheat oven to 375° F (190°C).
7. Place on a baking sheet, spacing logs slightly apart. Cover and let rise for another 30-45 minutes.
8. Bake buns for 15-18 minutes, or until golden brown.
9. Let cool on a wire rack before slicing.

SUKIYAKI

After heading south from Kawachinagano Station for a half-hour, Yamamoto-san squeezed down a one-lane road cut between two rice fields. The Suzuki pulled to a stop in front of Nanten-en, a Japanese *ryokan* inn—and my first home in Japan. Low, over-hanging pine branches framed Nanten-en's double-door entrance. Above, a traditional, slope-style tiled roof cut across the skyline. I grabbed my luggage, crossed the inn's red arch bridge, and stepped inside.

A *ryokan* has several distinct features. Typically, there is an *onsen*, Japan's traditional indoor bath. The *onsen* experience is a testimony to the country's emphasis on cleanliness and relaxation. Before entering the heated pool, you're expected to wash thoroughly; this scrub-down is so important that it often lasts longer than the bathing experience itself. Once clean, you climb into the water for a soak. Nudity is almost always implied.

Onsen culture is perfect for those looking to unwind for a weekend. It reflects the tranquility of Japan's countryside—sleep in, enjoy a fresh meal, relax in the hot springs, repeat.

Tradition is another *ryokan* staple. The history of Japan's home-style inns dates to the eighth century AD. Nishiyama Onsen Kei-unkan, a historic ryokan in Yamanashi Prefecture, is the oldest hotel in the world. (After a short 1,292 years in operation, the inn conceded to structural renovations in 1997.)

Tradition is everywhere in ryokans, and Nanten-en is no exception. Kingo Tatsuno, the world-class Japanese architect behind Tokyo Station and Tokyo Bank, designed the property in 1914. Today, the hotel is recognized as a part of Japan's cultural heritage.

Back in the entrance hall, I was immediately met by two staff members wearing kimonos. I removed my sneakers, slipped into a pair of XL caramel-colored sandals, and followed my hosts down the red-carpeted hallway.

My room at Nanten-en consisted of three smaller rooms, all covered in traditional tatami mats. In Japan, the 3x6 rice-strip tatami mat is a common unit of room measurement. Think the metric system is difficult? Try converting your dream Osaka apartment from tatami mats to square feet without a calculator.

There was a small entryway, a hanging closet, and a main room for writing and sleeping. Altogether, the space was eight tatami mats (okay, 144 sq. ft.). Very small, yes. But, in traditional *ryokan* style, the short-legged table, minimalist decorations, and light-flooded windows filled the room with a solid sense of depth.

A knock on the door broke my jetlagged daze. "Excuse me," the individual said in a perfect British accent.

I walked to the door, curious to see how *Downton Abbey* had infiltrated rural Osaka. I turned the handle and stood face-to-face—or rather, face-to-shoulders—with the tallest British man I'd ever seen in full kimono. Suddenly, it clicked. On the drive down from the airport, Yamamoto-san mentioned that the desk clerk at Nanten-en went by "Gary-san." Even with my rudimentary Japanese, I could recognize the foreign etymology at work in such a name.

"Are you Gary-san?" I asked.

"Yes. It's a pleasure to meet you," he said, whispering in a voice unexpectedly soft for his stature. "I've just come to inform you that dinner is ready."

Gary-san strolled off, hands clasped pensively behind his back. My questions would have to wait. It was time to eat.

My stay in early October, before COVID restrictions lifted and tourists returned to Japan, unfolded in a wonderful solitude. Every day, at exactly 8:00 a.m., 12:00 p.m., and 6:00 p.m., I dined at Nanten-en's banquet room. The outside scenery, a composition of red and yellow leaves peeking through layers of green, shone through floor-to-ceiling windows.

Seasonal awareness, known as *kisetsukan*, is a pillar of Japanese culture, and serious chefs will exert themselves to source the freshest fruit or the most seasonal fish. My meals reflected the inn's autumn scenery. For breakfast, fresh salmon, matsutake mushrooms, and sweet, starchy chestnuts accompanied ever-present bowls of white rice and miso soup. Lunch featured popular comfort foods, like tempura and curry rice, to stave off the growing chill of winter. Dinner, served in haute-cuisine, *kaiseki* style, included a course of tuna sashimi atop scarlet maple leaves, *takuan* (pickled radish), and a pear-persimmon dessert medley.

On my first morning at Nanten-en, Gary-san approached my table just as I finished my tea. He bowed, kneeled at the table's edge, and pulled out a thick brochure. A web-like map of historic walking trails covering the hills around Nanten-en unfolded across the breakfast table.

"I've done most of these," he said proudly. Gary-san, it turns out,

My meals reflected the inn's autumn scenery.

"季節感"
ki setsu kan

Mizuna greens &
Shimeji mushrooms
with soy sauce.

Grilled mackerel
with sweet
soy sauce
marinade.

Minched duck with
sugar, miso and
poppy seeds.

Ayu sweetfish
with roe.

Boiled & salted
Edamame.

Steamed glutinous
rice with chestnuts

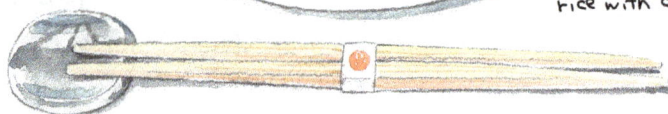

was somewhat of a local guide.

Apologizing for the brochure's lack of English, he scribbled a few ad-hoc translations. "Number 18, Kanii Shrine, is a favorite of mine," he said, pointing to a spot about a half kilometer away from Nanten-en. "Number 23 as well, Shugendo Pilgrimage point." Gary-san's voice grew more excited with each shortcut and trail.

"Oh, this is slightly wrong," he said, pointing to the location of a shrine in the bottom left corner of the map. He crossed it out in pen, redrawing the dot an inch higher. "It's more like here."

This red pen edit seemed to stir something in him. Freehand lines soon scored the entire brochure. Two dots appeared on the adjacent fold, indicating two more shrines on top of the introductory paragraph. The area's oldest nature trail appeared just west of the contact information. Almost none of his favorites were recorded on official maps, Gary-san told me.

"On good days, I take new ways home from work," he said. That is, instead of the usual twenty-five-minute commute back to Kawachinagano City, Gary-san sets off through Nanten-en's surrounding hills, taking anywhere between two to three hours to make it home.

"What did you do before this?" I asked.

"Video game development," he answered casually, as if rural expedition was the natural career pivot. "And before that, private banking."

The next day, after a dip in the *onsen*, I dressed and headed to the lobby. Okami-san, who served as the inn's day-to-day manager, stopped me as I slipped on my walking shoes. Draped in her crisp, blue-and-yellow kimono, Okami-san commanded total respect. I had witnessed her presence several times already throughout my stay. When she walked into a room, voices hushed. Shoulders straightened. Heads bowed in respect.

At dinner time, she invariably appeared by my table to introduce the evening's dishes before politely excusing herself, regretting that

SUKIYAKI

her schedule prevented her from joining me for the evening. Like countless guests before me, I was totally charmed.

As we stood in the lobby, Okami-san's frame barely leveled with my shoulders. She smiled and extended a small scrap of paper from her hand:

Please come to family dinner at 6:30 tonight

"Your family, my family. Dinner tonight," she said.

In Japan, families typically pass ryokans down family lines, generation by generation. Okami-san runs Nanten-en with her husband, Yamazaki-san, who inherited the inn from his father, Yamazaki Kiyoshi. Dinner with Okami-san's family was more than just a meal; it was a glimpse into the inn's past, present, and future.

After a day of exploring the countryside, I set off back to Nant-en-en. The late afternoon sun started to droop, illuminating the valley's cascading rice fields with a golden film. Gold was a reminder that summer was ending and the harvest was days away. I spotted a farmer in the distance, arms crossed, watching his rice crop like a child counting presents on Christmas Eve.

I crossed the inn's entryway and hurried back to my room. I was anxious to meet Yamazaki-san. Yamazaki Kiyoshi was one of Japan's most famous calligraphers, and Yamazaki-san had apparently inherited his father's artistic talent along with the property. The flower arrangements in each guest room were designed by Yamazaki-san himself, following the Japanese tradition of ikebana, or flower art. I racked my brain for dinner's potential conversation topics. I wasn't optimistic that he wanted to chat about the latest episode of *Love Island*.

At around 5:45 p.m., I showered, dipped in the *onsen*, and dressed. Wearing a black collared shirt, grey pants, and the only dress shoes I'd packed for Japan, I hoped my somewhat-formal attire compensated for fresh nerves and lingering jetlag.

As I approached the banquet room, two children, a boy and a girl, peeked around the entryway. I greeted them in limited Japanese—which I'm sure sounded hilarious—removed my shoes, and stepped onto the tatami floor. The room's usual bright autumn foliage was gone, replaced by sharp spotlights peeking through the darkness.

C Tatami mat flooring... No shoes allowed.

After a few prerequisite bows, I was introduced to my dinner company. The two young children were Yamazaki-san and Okami-san's grandkids, a brother-and-sister reception team.

To my right, I met Kazuki-san, Yamazaki-san and Okami-san's son and the heir-apparent to the Nanten-en legacy. He had long, dark hair and Yamazaki-san's easy smile. Kazuki-san introduced me to his wife, Asuka-san, sitting across the table next to their two-year-old son. The young couple's decision to join the family businesses wasn't always a foregone conclusion. Many friends their age rushed to leave Kawachinagano, moving an hour away to Osaka City, Japan's third-largest urban area. More still opted for the neon allure of Tokyo, less than three hours away via the Tokaido Shinkansen high-speed rail. Kazuki-san's older sister decided to pursue a PhD in Germany. By staying in Kawachinagano, Kazuki-san and Asuka-san were making a statement about tradition, family, and legacy. I asked Kazuki-san if he ever missed the pace of city life. "I tried to live in Yokohama a few years after school," he said. "It wasn't for me."

I sat farthest from the entrance, in the traditional place of honor, watching dinner's rich choreography unfold around the table. First, two members of the inn's staff placed identical cast-iron pots on portable gas stoves at either end of the table. They reemerged moments later, carrying several plates of vegetables—lettuce, mushrooms, and mung bean sprouts—with thick stacks of sliced wagyu. This was sukiyaki, one of Japan's most extravagant winter meals.

Confronted by the platter of wagyu, my mind froze. It couldn't be meat. In some sections, the beef's marbling was so dense it projected a single, soft shade of pink, taunting my eyes to find distinct hues of tissue and fat. It was an optical illusion. It was art.

"*Itadakimasu,*" the table recited in unison, hands together in prayer-like fashion. The gas stovetops shot to life. Wielding long, wooden chopsticks, Yamazaki-san plucked a thick fat cube from the plate and pressed it into the cast iron pot. Kazuki-san mirrored his father's technique on the second pot, filling the room with a sizzling chorus. Once his pot was hot enough, Yamazaki-san placed four slices of wagyu onto the bubbling fat, pushing them around with his chopsticks. Okami-san joined in, sprinkling sugar crystals over the meat before melting them down with soy sauce. "Sweet and salty," she said.

The brown glaze started to bubble. I couldn't wait much longer. Yamazaki-san smiled, gave a final, knowing stir, and placed a massive slice of wagyu in my bowl.

Can a single bite be life-changing? That's a question with no clear answer. I think my first oyster was. I'd say that food can be moving in the same way as a Gustav Klimt painting or a Nina Simone song. But my first taste of sukiyaki reached another place entirely. My mind went blank, like a computer zapped by a sudden overload of energy. There was no miraculous, Ratatouille-like moment of transporting to a place in my memory. I didn't have anywhere to go, no reference to localize my feelings at that moment.

I tried to articulate myself to Yamazaki-san and Okami-san, who were busy stirring mushrooms, lettuce, and tofu around with the remaining meat. "Wow. It melts." That's all I could summon. The

fresh wagyu, encrusted in sizzling fat, sugar, and soy sauce, dripped juice down my mouth.

Yamazaki-san laughed knowingly. When he laughed, he clenched his teeth together and shut his eyes, like he had just stubbed his toe. Switching to English for the first time all night, Yamazaki-san raised an all-important question. "Would you like to try Japanese saké?"

My family dinner at Nanten-en is the most special meal I've ever had. Initially, I was anxious, the foreign guest at the owners' table. But it wasn't like that—no awkward disconnect between me and Yamazaki-san, no silent stares from Okami-san. We shared a love of good food and, more specifically, good food eaten together.

Weeks later, while studying the term sukiyaki in a Japanese class, I realized a mistake. I already knew *yaki* translated to "grilled," but I had the wrong definition of *suki*. I thought *sukiyaki* translated to "favorite dish grilled." The actual translation is "grilled on a plowshare," referring to the traditional Buddhist custom of grilling meat outside.

I wasn't even close. But, in a way, I like my translation better. Suki-yaki really is that simple. It's the best thing you can find cooked in a hot, cast-iron glaze of fat, sugar, and soy sauce. But what makes it my favorite is how you eat it: surrounded by family and friends, all cooking for each other, right on the table. That's sukiyaki. And I'll take my Nanten-en translation over standard Japanese any day.

SUKIYAKI

INGREDIENTS

- 1/2 lb (225g) thinly sliced beef (ribeye or sirloin)
- 1 tablespoon vegetable oil
- 1/2 onion, sliced
- 4 shiitake mushrooms, stems removed and sliced
- 1/2 cup napa cabbage, chopped
- 2 green onions, chopped into 2-inch pieces
- 1 small carrot, thinly sliced
- 1 cup dashi stock (or water)

Sauce Ingredients

- 1/4 cup soy sauce
- 1/4 cup mirin
- 2 tablespoons sake
- 1 tablespoon sugar

INSTRUCTIONS

1. In a small bowl, mix soy sauce, mirin, sake, and sugar to make the sukiyaki sauce.
2. Heat oil in a large skillet or shallow pot over medium heat. Add onion and cook until softened.
3. Add beef slices and cook until lightly browned. Pour in the sauce.
4. Add mushrooms, tofu, cabbage, shirataki noodles, green onions, and carrot. Pour in dashi stock.
5. Cover and simmer for 5-7 minutes, allowing flavors to meld.
6. Serve directly from the pot, placing the beef and vegetables over rice if desired.

SHORT RIBS

Hotel Carmichael, the 122-room hotel built between the Palladium and the shops in Carmel City Center, is one of the few places in Indiana that can pull off a nightly champagne toast. Its interior is a hypnotic pattern of polished black-and-white tile. The hotel's west wing, carved in balconies and patios, overlooks the Monon Trail, Carter Green, and the Palladium's limestone exterior. Hotel Carmichael even boasts its own French restaurant, Vivante, just one marble staircase away (assuming you're already in the lobby for the champagne toast).

With a presence so large, bordering on grandeur, how can anything feel local? How can the hotel retain its sense of place?

The answer is in the food. That became obvious when I met Jason Crouch, the executive chef of Vivante. Both big and tall, with a well-trimmed beard that framed his otherwise unadorned head, Crouch moves with the intensity of a man who knows the exact difference, in milliseconds, between rare and medium rare. He caught my hand with a quick shake and started out toward Vivante's brick patio.

This intensity drives Crouch's approach to food and its place in the community. He grew up on a farm in Muncie, Indiana, just about an hour from Carmel. When he talks about Vivante, he repeats words like simple and local. He talks about relationships. For Crouch, Indiana's food culture is about knowing where ingredi-

ents come from. Knowing faces, families, and first names.

This philosophy, sparked by his childhood and forged through years of culinary school, is how Crouch connects Hotel Carmichael to Carmel. Wake up early enough, and you may just see him wheeling his red wagon around the Carmel Farmers Market on Saturday mornings. The fresh strawberries and brussels sprouts aren't for his day off—they're next week's menu at Vivante.

CHEF CROUCH'S SHORT RIBS

(Makes 10 servings)

INGREDIENTS

- 4 lbs. beef short ribs
- 1 cup bourbon
- 1 pt. beef stock
- 4 oz. tomato paste
- 1 cup hot mustard
- 1 cup molasses
- 1/2 cup apple cider vinegar
- 1/4 cup onion powder
- 1/8 cup fresh garlic
- 1 qt. worcestershire sauce
- Salt and pepper as preferred

INSTRUCTIONS

1. Cut short ribs into 6 oz. portions.
2. Season with salt and pepper.
3. Sear ribs on high heat on all sides and place in a casserole dish.
4. Mix remaining ingredients in a bowl and whisk until combined.
5. Pour mixture over ribs, cover casserole dish with aluminum foil, and bake at 210° F (100° C) for six hours.
6. Remove cooked ribs from liquid and slide bones out of the meat (should occur easily).
7. Reduce the liquid in a pot over low heat until it thickens and sticks to a spoon.
8. Place ribs on a serving plate and cover with the reduced sauce.

CURRY RICE

A well-made plate of curry rice can change your life. Or, at the very least, it can leave you with a warm stomach and enough energy to stay motivated while you change your life. It's rich, flavorful, and familiar in the way all comfort food should feel familiar. Since coming back from Kawachinagano, I've committed the recipe to memory—I can't risk losing it in my Notes app.

The history of curry rice (*kare raisu*) mirrors the history of Japan itself. During the Meiji era (1868–1912), the British Navy brought cumin, turmeric, and other spices to the island in the form of thick, cafeteria-style curry. The flavors caught on quickly. Around the same time, Japanese farmers began growing carrots, potatoes, and onions alongside their standard rice crops. Local chefs utilized said crops, as well as new proteins like beef and chicken, to adopt the Navy's curry recipe for local restaurants and cookbooks. Today, it's a national dish in Japan—people consume more curry than sushi or tempura. And its maritime roots remain strong. Japan's Self-Defense Force eats *kaigun kare* (literally "navy curry") every Friday.

But curry is more than just a way to tell time at sea. For many, it's the taste of nostalgia. A flashback to stepping in from the winter air, hearing a voice call *"Okaeri!"* (You're back!) from the kitchen, and watching the steam rise off a bowl of curry, potatoes, and beef. For others, it's the chance to reclaim a Western import. Curry udon, curry ramen, and curry buns (*kare pan*) all represent Japa-

nese variations on the original Meiji era import.

I wouldn't call curry fast food, even though CoCo Ichibanya, the country's most popular curry chain, has over 1,200 locations across Japan. I would call it convenience food. Almost every recipe starts with a hard block of instant curry, melted down and stirred into a brown roux. Purists even insist that if it's not made with a curry block, it's not real Japanese curry. I see their point. Cooking for thirty? No need to scale the spice ratios—just break off a few more blocks.

CURRY RICE

(Makes 4 servings)

INGREDIENTS

○ 1 tablespoon vegetable oil
○ 1 pound boneless chicken thighs, cut into bite-sized pieces
○ 1 onion, sliced
○ 2 carrots, peeled and chopped
○ 1 potato, peeled and diced
○ 3 cups water
○ 1 package (3.5 oz) Japanese curry roux (I like Golden curry)
○ 1 teaspoon soy sauce
○ 1 teaspoon honey
○ 4 cups cooked short-grain rice

INSTRUCTIONS

① Heat vegetable oil in large pot over medium heat. Add the chicken and cook until browned on all sides. Add the onions and sauté until softened.

② Stir in carrots and potatoes, cooking for another 2 minutes. Pour in water and bring to a boil. Reduce heat to low and simmer for 15-20 minutes, until vegetables are tender.

③ Break curry roux into cubes and stir into pot until fully dissolved. Add soy sauce and honey if using. Simmer for 5 more minutes, stirring occasionally, until the curry thickens.

④ Serve the curry over bowls of warm rice.

CHEESEBURGER

The exterior of Bub's Burgers and Ice Cream is instantly charming, with honeysuckle yellow siding and dark green trim adorning the front porch. Nearby, a sprawling patio runs parallel to the main stretch of the Monon Trail. This trailside location guarantees a constant stream of foot traffic, and many disciplined runners have found themselves drifting from the Monon toward the wafting smell of a Bub's cheeseburger.

The walls inside Bub's reveal a different story. Not of warm neighborhood evenings in Anytown, USA, but of Herculean myth. The floor-to-ceiling wallpaper is in fact not wallpaper, at least not in a traditional sense. The walls are covered in 4 x 6 photographs, all shot with the same blinding camera flash. A plaque hangs halfway up one of the walls:

"CHAMPIONS
OF THE
BIG UGLY"

This is the legend of Bub's Burgers and Ice Cream. The beast at the center of any Carmel foodie's journey to glory.

The Big Ugly Cheeseburger starts with 22 ounces of uncooked grass-fed beef—about as heavy as a basketball. It's grilled down to 16 ounces, topped with three slices of cheese, and pushed between a half-pound bun. Finish the burger, and your photo joins its fellow finishers on the restaurant's photo wall.

But even the wall of CHAMPIONS is not without hierarchy. Eat a Big Ugly, get a 4x6 photo on the wall. Eat two Big Uglies (Ugli?) and get an 8x10. The third Big Ugly, in my analysis, is what separates the professionals from the amateurs. Eating more than two Big Uglies is personally hard to conceptualize, in the same way it's hard to see myself throwing a basketball off a backboard, catching it mid-360-degree spin, and dunking it with both hands. Three Big Uglies earns you a poster on the wall. Only four people have eaten four Big Uglies. In 2023, James Webb, an Australian professionally ranked in Major League Eating (yes), ate six Big Uglies in thirty-seven minutes.

I set out to get my photo on the wall. My preparation—in the loosest sense of the word—consisted of a light lunch and two sets of tennis. I was physically, emotionally, and metabolically ready for the Big Ugly.

The burger is just about 1½ iPhones wide—far too wide to eat without cutting it down the middle. A proud eater must put his machismo aside in such practical matters. Lifting half of the Big Ugly to my mouth with both hands, I fully understood why finishers earn a spot on the wall. The 16-ounce burger feels more like sheer mass than weight. Thankfully, its size notwithstanding, the beast has one vulnerability: it tastes amazing. It's the type of burger you can't put down—assuming your forearms are up to the workout. The meat is juicy, the lettuce crisp, and the half-pound homemade bun ties everything together. I experienced what's known to runners as a negative split—meaning I ate the second half of my Big Ugly faster than the first. I posed for my 4x6 just as the sun slipped under the skyline. It was a tasty deal for photo wall immortality.

CHEESEBURGER

(Makes 4 burgers)

INGREDIENTS

- 1 pound ground beef
- 1 teaspoon salt
- 1/2 teaspoon black pepper
- 1/2 teaspoon garlic powder
- 4 slices cheddar cheese
- 4 hamburger buns
- 1 tablespoon butter, melted

INSTRUCTIONS

① Preheat grill or skillet to medium-high heat.

② In a bowl, mix the ground beef with salt, black pepper, and garlic powder. Divide mixture into four equal portions. Shape each into a patty, pressing a small indentation in the center.

③ Place patties on grill or skillet. Cook for 3-4 minutes on one side. Flip and cook for another 3-4 minutes. In last minute of cooking, place a slice of cheese on each patty. Cover grill or pan until cheese melts.

④ Brush buns with melted butter. Toast them in skillet or on grill until golden brown. Assemble the burgers with desired toppings (lettuce, tomato, pickles, etc) and serve.

OKONOMIYAKI

Let me just say it upfront: I'm biased. Okonomiyaki is my favorite food in Japan. But if you spent a month living in Kawachinagano with the Tsunamotos, tucked in their front yard guesthouse, mixing homemade okonomiyaki batter and eating roasted ginkgo nuts, I'm pretty sure it would be your favorite food, too.

The first family member I met was Chibi, the giant rooster guarding the Tsunamotos' front yard. Yamamoto-san and I stood outside the front door, luggage in hand, attempting to avoid the clearly territorial rooster's attention. The door slid open, revealing a middle-aged man with glasses and a blue flannel shirt. He said hello, gestured a formal bow, and let out a small, nervous laugh when he saw Chibi lurking around the yard. This was Takeo-san, the father of the Tsunamoto family—and the illustrator of this book.

I met Takeo's wife, Koto-san, that afternoon. Takeo-san was born in Japan but grew up in the Netherlands. Koto-san (named after tennis star Margaret Court) was born and raised forty-five minutes from Kawachinagano in north Osaka.

Takeo-san is an artist with the quiet humility that comes from having both serious talent and public recognition. One weekend, we were walking through Osaka City's Tenjinbashi neighborhood when we saw a poster for the Osaka Museum of Housing and Living. The poster, Koto-san told me, was Takeo-san's design. I made him stop and pose for a photo.

Koto-san works with an energy and passion that makes the fact that she has several jobs seem completely normal and almost inadequate. She's on the preservation team at Osaka's Municipal Housing Corporation, and mentors young architecture students at Osaka Public University. She and Takeo-san cook together, too, splitting time on the kitchen stereo between Nina Simone and Rush.

The Tsunamotos have two children: Shin and Chisae. Both are funny and earnest and currently in that young adult phase where you're not supposed to actually like your parents. Shin models black, exclusive-looking clothing and has followers on Instagram to prove it. Chisae and I built an elaborate banter around the twenty words we knew between Japanese and English. Almost half were K-pop groups and SpongeBob characters.

All this to say the Tsunamotos are decent people. Which made nightly dinners, sitting around their *chabudai*-style table, really wonderful. We ate together, all five of us. Always with miso soup. And always with a bowl of white rice.

Okonomiyaki is a classic Osaka food: messy, rich, and unpretentious. The image that sticks with me is a savory pancake held together by flour, eggs, and cabbage. It is not a pretty food—even topped with an intricate lace of brown okonomiyaki sauce and mayonnaise. But looks and taste are not the same thing. Okonomiyaki tastes great, like you threw together every leftover in your fridge and fried it over a griddle. The name combines the term *yaki*, meaning "grilled" or "fried," and *okonomi*, meaning "what you like." As long as it binds and fries, anything goes.

The Tsunamotos gave me two presents before I left Japan. One was a square-shaped pan for cooking tamagoyaki, Japan's classic rolled omelet. The other was okonomiyaki sauce.

I tried and failed to recreate the dish at home. Nothing could substitute for Takeo-san's humor or Koto-san's warmth. That's the secret to good okonomiyaki: who's around the table is just as important as the ingredients inside.

That may be the dish's secret:
Who's around the table is just as important as
the ingredients inside.

OKONOMIYAKI

(Makes 2 large pancakes)

INGREDIENTS

- 1 cup all-purpose flour
- 1/2 cup dashi stock (or water)
- 1 teaspoon baking powder
- 1 egg
- 2 cups cabbage, finely shredded
- 1/4 cup green onions, chopped
- 1/2 cup cooked bacon or thinly sliced pork belly
- 1/4 cup tempura bits (optional)

For Toppings

- Okonomiyaki sauce
- Mayo
- Bonito flakes
- Pickled ginger

① In a bowl, whisk together flour, dashi stock, and baking powder until smooth.

② Add the egg, cabbage, green onions, and tempura bits, mixing gently until combined.

③ Heat a griddle or lightly oiled pan over medium heat. Pour half of the batter into the pan, shaping it into a round pancake.

④ Place bacon or pork belly slices on top. cover and cook for about 4-5 minutes.

⑤ Flip carefully and cook for another 4-5 minutes until golden brown and fully cooked.

⑥ Transfer to a plate and drizzle with okonomi-yaki sauce and mayo. Sprinkle with bonito flakes and pickled ginger.

⑦ Repeat for the second pancake and serve hot.

GARLIC BUTTER STEAK

My alarm sounded at 2:15 a.m. Time to go. The Carmel Farmers Market starts every Saturday at 8:00 a.m. But, for another group, the market starts much earlier—around 4:00 a.m. I was awake to join that world.

Becker Family Farms started coming to Carmel's Farmers Market over ten years ago. Every Saturday, Kyle Becker, flanked by a small crew that includes his four children, loads beef, pork, chicken, turkey, veal, milk, and eggs into a trailer and begins his drive from Mooreland, Indiana, to Carmel's Carter Green. A decade of practice does not render the fifty-five-mile drive any shorter.

I left Carmel just before 3:00 a.m. I merged onto I-69 and met two early companions: a black SUV—which may be the only car you'd expect to see at that hour—and the flushed glow of Top Golf's LED lights sprawling onto the interstate. The entire drive to Mooreland became a descent deeper into Indiana: onto I-69 N, past Pendleton, past Nestle's giant, silver-back bunny mascot in Anderson, exit to State Road 109, and finally, a twenty-five-mile straight away on US-36 E.

The farm was about fifty yards north of its Google Maps pin, Kyle told me earlier on the phone. I would've caught the error intuitively; in the darkness, the hum of white floodlights worked better than any navigation app. I pulled into the side lot, dragging dust into the air as I wedged between two tractor trailers. The main farmhouse was already awake with activity. Groggy faces bobbed in and out of the walk-in freezer, carrying boxes marked "Chicken Eggs" and "Cow Milk." It was 3:55 a.m.—I was behind schedule, and the operation had already started.

I grabbed my camera, hopped out of the car, and walked over to the action. A thin, middle-aged man in an Indianapolis Colts hoodie greeted me as I reached the farmhouse door. "Mornin!" he said with the energy of someone regularly awake before sunrise.

Brian, as he introduced himself between trips to the walk-in, lived in Mooresville and worked with Kyle at the Carmel market. His

sixteen-year-old son, Trey, helped out, too, at least until school started in the fall. I followed the father-son duo into the farmhouse, pausing to avoid two grey kittens roaming near the entrance.

Wearing a tucked-in Becker Farms T-shirt, cargo shorts, and muddied work boots, Kyle looked unmistakably in charge. He was deep in thought, typing on a tiny pocket calculator cradled in his callused hands. Brian, Trey, and I waited near the entryway. He was tallying boxes, first of eggs and then pork shoulder, Brian explained. It was part of a sleek efficiency I recognized throughout the farm's early-morning routine. The work flowed like a countdown to 5:15 a.m. Kyle's team moved with tight choreography, only pausing to crack the occasional joke or redirect a wandering calf.

The scene would be overstimulating at any hour. But, at 4:30 a.m., my senses were especially shot. Along the dirt-covered driveway, a swarm of maybe fifteen cats, many of them kittens, skirted out from under tractor supplies and compost piles. Kyle's young daughters, Charlotte and Stella, took turns leading the family's black calf on a morning walk. After establishing the immediate—the calf's name was Baby (what are the top 100 calf names?)—I turned to the more existential. Why were the girls awake before 5:00 a.m. on a Saturday? "We're doing morning chores," Charlotte replied.

The girls finished walking Baby and started off to the animal stables near the farmhouse. I followed behind. In the darkness, I stepped over patches of hay-scattered mud, still fresh from rain earlier that week. The wafting smell of farm animals dampened Indiana's early morning air. As I quickly learned, sight was not enough. Becker Farms was to be understood through a variety of senses.

Everything in sight, from the stable walls to the mud floors, was illuminated by a weak shade of yellow light against the darkness. I heard a sudden, high-pitched squeal from the ground to my immediate left and leaped back about five yards, barely catching my

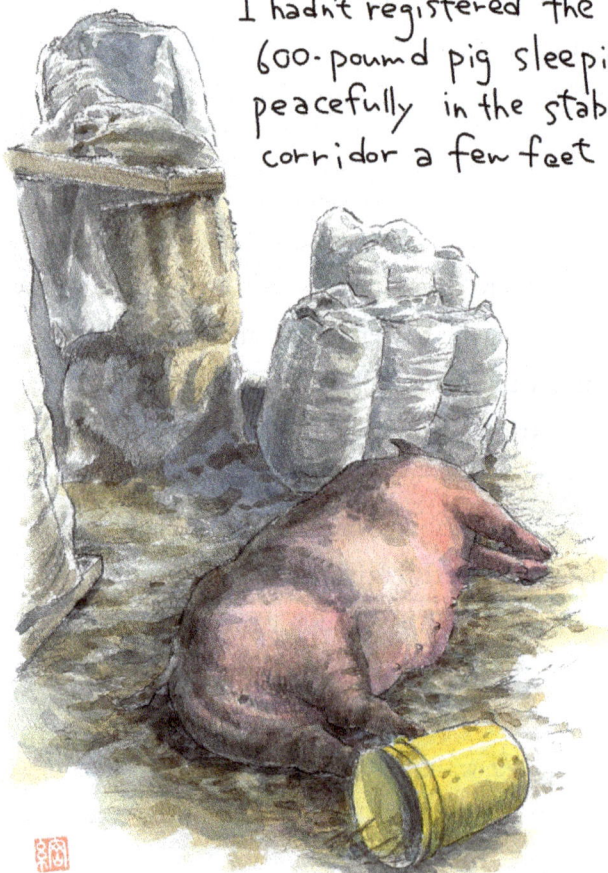

I hadn't registered the 600-pound pig sleeping peacefully in the stable corridor a few feet away.

balance while my camera swung wildly around my neck. I heard Charlotte and Stella laughing behind me.

I never saw the six hundred-pound pig sleeping peacefully inches away from my feet. My eyes registered the massive animal, of course. But, in the dull yellow light, my brain cataloged it as a pinkish, yellowish lump. I had never seen a pig so large with my own eyes.

I trekked deeper into Becker Farms while the girls poured breakfast into the pig stable. Several more pigs, albeit none quite as large, rushed to join the feeding frenzy. Away from the loading docks, I realized how dark the sky looked. The sun wouldn't rise for another hour. For a moment, I just stood there, neck craned skyward. I could make out Kyle's figure in the distance, stacking coolers into the trailer. Except for an occasional laugh carrying across the stable, the field was completely still.

I crossed back through the stable. Kyle emerged from the farm's walk-in freezer, carrying the last carton of eggs under his arm. We gathered around the trailer for a final rundown. Becker Farms, like most Indiana vendors, provided goods to multiple markets across the state.

Kyle quickly walked through the morning's tactics. Brian, his second-in-command, would make an initial drop-off at Noblesville, around twenty miles from Carmel, and then rejoin Kyle at the Carmel market. Brian slurped his 64-oz Big Gulp—done. Kyle

would head straight to Carmel, using the extra hour to assemble the farm's tents and folding tables. Stella would join for logistics and moral support.

The whole pre-departure meeting took about ninety seconds. It was already 5:16 a.m.—go-time. I waved goodbye to Stella, got back into my car, and began the journey back to Carmel, watching the red dots of Kyle's taillights against the faint blue morning.

The sun climbed up my rear-view mirror, illuminating the growing stream of cars on US-36. It was no longer a lonely commute. Kyle, keeping with the tradition of Midwest dads before him, insisted that there would be no rest stops on the drive from Mooreland. "No coffee?" I asked, hoping I sounded more professionally curious than personally invested. "Nope, no time," Kyle said. There were no last-minute itinerary changes in the Becker Farms handbook. After watching Kyle's morning routine, I found it hard to object.

The sky was a sheet of orange by the time we reached Carmel. I felt an odd familiarity driving down Main Street, onto Rangeline, and finally down 126th Street to the Palladium and Carter Green, where the Carmel Farmers Market is held each weekend. It was the same route I took to the market with my family. After following behind Kyle and Stella for fifty-five miles, my five-minute commute felt luxurious.

This was the real effort it took to produce the market. It didn't magically appear every Saturday morning. Vendors like Becker Farms, which are just people like Kyle and Stella, worked for days to create the thirty-second experience of buying a few steaks or two dozen eggs. It's an unequal dynamic—one that may only be balanced by constant gratitude from the market's supporters.

Kyle and Stella arrived at Carter Green and began assembling Becker Farms' booth. Kyle had clearly memorized the process: the tension of the interlocking tent legs, the snap of the collapsible table, the exact dimensions of his tabletop coolers. The set-up process was older than Stella herself. Nonetheless, she followed along with studied fluency. The father-daughter team fastened their final zip ties around 7:30 a.m., a full half hour before opening.

The market started to murmur around 8:15 a.m. Visitors passed through the aisles of vendor booths, stopping to glance at the seasonal colors of produce along their route. Most adhered to an early-morning hierarchy of needs. First, find a coffee. After acquiring their cold brew, these 8:05-8:30 a.m. arrivals brightened up, taking time to explore each tent and exchange greetings with the vendors.

I finished my initial loop around the market and headed back to the Becker Farms booth by 8:40 a.m. Kyle looked comfortable behind his fleet of coolers. He had opted for a subtle wardrobe change, throwing a flannel button-down over his Becker Farms work shirt. Plastic bags hung off his jean pockets, ready for quick-draw order fulfillment.

The checkout process was, in true Becker Farms fashion, a sleek, efficient routine: Once a customer made her selection—pork, beef, or eggs—Stella grabbed a plastic bag and filled it accordingly, tying it between the handle loops and passing it down to Kyle. Kyle weighed the goods, performed a final quality inspection, and provided some light checkout banter.

Kyle wasn't a salesman. At least not in the typical, car dealership sense of the word. He had phrases he would throw out from his own language of situational cues to respond to customers. "You betcha," was a common affirmation. So was "awesome sauce." Periodically, customers approached the booth and gravitated toward him. "I have a question for you," they would start. "I got an answer," Kyle would shoot back.

The next evening, I pulled out two fresh Becker Farms steaks for Father's Day. Kyle's instructions sat open in the Notes app of my phone. My dad seasoned the meat with salt and pepper as I flicked on the grill's propane tank. Like many American families, our backyard grill carried significance beyond food. More than the perfect burger or steak, grilling had become a place for moments of small conversation and shared time in the backyard.

Juicy, sizzling fat dripped beneath the grill's cast-iron grates as a pair of tongs guided the steaks onto a cutting board. I recalled Kyle's adamant advice on this stage of the grilling process: Steaks needed to rest for at least five minutes before any cutting. When cooked at a high temperature, the protein fibers in the meat push its juices toward the center of the cut. If you cut a steak immediately after cooking it, all the juices, all the moisture, immediately pour out, creating an unappetizing mess—not to mention a huge loss of flavor. Steaks were not to be disrespected in such a manner. I took over for my dad, spooning on Kyle's signature homemade garlic butter and watching it melt over the two gigantic steaks.

Fresh beef from Becker Farms.

Grilled to medium rare perfection.

Juicy, tender, and dripping with flavor.

Spoonful of garlic butter.

Five minutes felt like an hour as the sweet, garlicky aroma of fresh-grilled steak wafted through the backyard. Finally, my phone's alarm sounded from the patio table. It was time to try the meat. The juicy pink interior was a perfect medium rare—not only my personal preference but also Kyle's professional recommendation. After a weekend of early morning wake-ups, long drives, and farmers market interviews, I felt a new appreciation for the meat in front of me.

The steak was delicious—juicy, tender, and dripping with flavor. Encrusted in salt, pepper, and melted garlic butter, it was an unadorned bite of mouth-watering perfection. But, like most transcendent food experiences, the steak was part of a larger weekend of happiness, a moment it held alongside summer, family, and community. I was back in Carmel, reunited with my parents, eating a steak straight from Kyle's farm. That's a flavor food alone can't bring, one you can't find in a cookbook.

GARLIC BUTTER STEAK

(Makes 1 steak)

INGREDIENTS

Steak

○ 1 8oz-10oz beef steak
○ 1 1/2 teaspoons salt
○ 2 teaspoons pepper

Garlic Butter

○ 1 tablespoon minced garlic (about 3 cloves),
○ 1/2 cup salted butter (softened)
○ 1 tablespoon parsley, finely chopped

Directions

① Remove steak from refrigerator 30 minutes prior to grilling. Sprinkle both sides evenly with salt and pepper.

② Set grill to medium-high heat (about 450° F), close the lid, and allow it to preheat (around 15 minutes).

③ In a small bowl, stir together butter, garlic, and parsley until well-combined. Set aside near grill.

④ Place the steak on grill grate and cook for approximately 3.5 minutes per side for medium rare finish, or until the steak's internal temperature reaches 135° F.

⑤ Pull the cooked steak off the grill and gently place it on a flat plate or cutting board.

⑥ Place 1 tablespoon of garlic butter mixture on top of the steak and let it rest for 5-6 minutes.

⑦ Cut and serve immediately.

CREAM ALE

The idea that teachers don't live at school sounds like an obvious one. But there they were, every morning around 7:30 a.m., at Carmel High School. It's an odd way to know someone. Entire relationships, sometimes spanning years, only existing inside a particular room.

When I started writing this book, I wanted to challenge myself. I hadn't kept in touch with my teachers, and the email threads I'd started after graduation deteriorated as I got further away from Carmel. But my English teacher, Mr. Love, still meant a lot to me. His classes had an authenticity that didn't transcribe easily onto a syllabus. We exchanged a few emails right after I graduated, and I periodically saw his updates on Facebook. I hated the idea that years of mentorship might be reduced to an unexpected run-in at the grocery store.

I sent him a Facebook message. My rambling invitation was quite simple: Let's meet up and reminisce.

We chose to meet at Carmel's Midtown Plaza, an oasis along the Monon Trail with a steady flow of bikes, joggers, and dogs. The 14,000 square-foot plaza, which finished construction in 2019, embodies a vision of Carmel defined by community. A patch of grass in the middle of the plaza, about the dimensions of a tennis court, offers space for friendly games of soccer, football, and freeze tag.

Blue umbrella-topped tables line the grass's perimeter, occasionally reinforcing the field's boundaries. Other features adorn the space: a notoriously expensive fire pit, a 16x14 television screen, and a metal ping-pong table decorated with Carmel's signature roundabouts.

I showed up to Midtown early, taking a quick lap around the grass to check out the space. It really was spectacular, even if a bit too perfect. An Allied Solutions sign hung above the plaza, highlighting the company's new presence in the neighborhood. To the left, Sun King Brewery offered an outdoor patio and a wide variety of house-made beers. Rows of apartment buildings, finished in anticipation of Midtown's revival, lined the patio's intersection with the Monon. You could easily go without a car here. Just in case, the south facade boasted a four-story, 308-space parking garage.

I found an open table along Sun King's red-brick patio. The late-summer sun dipped behind a row of shops across the street, throwing a long, lazy shadow along the plaza's edge.

A few minutes later, Mr. Love walked through the far end of Midtown, looking like the same guy who had handed me a diploma five years earlier. His thick-rimmed glasses and long gray beard— trademarks of his time in the English department—still carried a sense of academic gravitas. But there was something else now, too.

He wore a vintage Coca-Cola long sleeve (untucked, of course), faded Levis, and a pair of red and white Nike Dunks. I was suddenly aware of my dirty Air Force 1s and wrinkled IU T-shirt.

For the first few minutes, our reunion felt very "run-in at the grocery store"-like. We exchanged rehearsed greetings. The shoes, he explained, noticing my stare, were part of a themed 1970s outfit for Homecoming Week. Still very cool.

But soon, the initial awkwardness faded. There was local beer in front of us. A late-summer breeze drifted through the plaza. Evening dog walkers strolled down the Monon Trail. Frankly, we were happy just to be outside.

"Do you miss the student interaction?" I asked him. Mr. Love had recently left the English department to work full-time in the school's library. "One hundred percent," he said quickly. "It's what I miss the most." He paused, then took a sip from his drink.

"I mean, you know how I was in the classroom," he said. "We'd tell jokes, we'd tell stories, I'd talk about my life. And, of course, academics were important, but I don't know . . ." he trailed off. "I don't have the basis to judge how it is now."

"It was the grading," he admitted. "I would come home from work, eat dinner, and then grade papers until I went to bed. Four or five nights a week." There was a melancholy tone to his voice but no regret.

And, besides, that was the past. We toasted his new position in the library. A good conversation over quality beer was reason enough to celebrate.

Sun King's Sunlight Cream Ale wasn't just quality by our standards. In 2015, just six years after founders Dave Colt and Clay Robinson rolled Sun King's first keg out of its Indianapolis distillery, the beer won a gold medal at the Great American Beer Festival in Colorado.

We talked for almost two hours. I no longer saw him as the invincible English teacher. He no longer saw me as the self-assured, National Honor Society-type. The curtain may have disappeared, but Mr. Love was still standing there, doing his best.

"I started bartending a few years ago, actually," he said as we finished our drinks and said goodbye. "It's sorta like teaching."

"How so?" I asked.

"Crowd control, mainly," he said, waving goodbye.

DESSERT

PERSIMMON PUDDING

The best desserts exude a familiar, nostalgic charm. You make chocolate cake expecting the rich flavor of chocolate. Apple pie tastes like apples, albeit especially buttery and sweet ones. But then, how can we place something like persimmon pudding? It's certainly timeless in Indiana. Carmel, too. But is that enough to say? Does it taste . . . persimmon-y?

I won't lie here. I'd never heard of persimmon pudding before I began this book. But the name kept sneaking up in conversation. I knew the recipe needed its recognition. I didn't expect, however, that the dessert would transport me through the history of Carmel—and the city's ties with Kawachinagano.

I first encountered the recipe at Carmel's International Arts Festival. I was introducing myself to the sister city volunteers and mentioned my idea for a Carmel-Kawachinagano cookbook. One of the volunteers, Mindy, looked rightfully concerned. She had lived in Japan after graduating from Earlham over thirty years ago, working in television, marketing, and several other professional roles that solidified an expert understanding of language and culture. She realized, probably even before I did, that this project was not a small undertaking.

Mindy pressed me on the details of the project ahead. Where would I stay in Kawachinagano? Did I speak Japanese? How did I plan to conduct my research? I addressed her points, trying to divert the conversation from its approaching vote of no confidence. Mindy nodded. Still skeptical, she posed her final question: You're planning to include a persimmon pudding recipe, right?

Prior to the festival, I knew Mindy only through her family's involvement in the Carmel-Kawachinagano relationship. Jerry and Kay, Mindy's parents, are longtime members of Carmel's sister cities association. If someone from Kawachinagano has seen Carmel over the past twenty-five years, there's a good chance they've eaten dinner with Mindy, Jerry, and Kay at the Myers' home.

A few months later, I drove up to the Myers property. The house sits on what remains of the family farm, tucked away in East Carmel between Main Street and 146th Street. Mindy greeted me under the long row of black walnut trees lining the driveway. "Konichiwa," she said, waving, and showed me up the porch steps. I met Jerry and Kay in the living room off the entryway. They were lovely and generous and as hospitable as you'd imagine a couple who regularly open their home to strangers would be. Jerry sat in a green recliner, Kay joined Mindy on the couch, and I took a corner chair facing the family.

Mindy's family has lived in Carmel since the 1830s. As in horse and wagon 1830s. Their history is tied to the history of the city. And when Kay handed me a faded, cursive index card titled "PERSIMMON PUDDING" from 1903, I couldn't help but think their family recipe was part of the city, too. The ingredients may have changed, but the taste remains the same.

The Myers make their pudding from persimmon trees that Jerry's father planted on the property over fifty years ago. When it's all mixed and emerging from the oven, you can smell the difference. The dessert wafts through the kitchen with a rich, holiday-like aroma. The taste, with a light tanginess from the persimmon pulp, is undeniably buttery. Texture-wise, it's somewhere between crème brûlée and gingerbread.

And yes, I'm here to confirm, it does in fact taste like persimmons—in the same way apple pie still tastes like apples. It's timeless. A dessert just as much Carmel as the family who started baking it over one hundred years ago.

PERSIMMON PUDDING

(Makes 16-20 servings)

INGREDIENTS

- 4 eggs
- 2 1/2 cups sugar
- 4 cups persimmon pulp
- 1 quart milk
- 2 cups flour
- 1 teaspoon baking soda
- 1 teaspoon baking powder
- 1 teaspoon salt

INSTRUCTIONS

1. Preheat the oven to 350° F.
2. In a large bowl, gently beat together the eggs.
3. Add the sugar and persimmon pulp to the egg mixture.
4. Stir in milk and mix the combination well.
5. Gradually add the flour, baking soda, baking powder, and salt.
6. Place in the oven and stir mixture periodically while baking.
7. Bake at 350° F until dark brown (approx. 60-90 minutes).

STRAWBERRY PIZZA

Kawachinagano has no shortage of farmland. Small, golden fields of rice sit behind almost every corner. And there are greens, too. The Osaka countryside is full of life.

During my first week in Kawachinagano, I visited a specialized pear farm about thirty minutes outside the city. The orchard utilizes mesh-wire netting, strung six feet off the ground, to brace its pear trees. Farmers twine each tree branch around the wire, allowing dense, softball-sized pears to grow without weighing down the trees. Another farm, run by identical twin brothers, sat alongside a creek in the shade of Kawachinagano's sloping mountainside. I've never seen tomatoes with such a deep red glow.

But my favorite farm in Kawachinagano belongs to Iisaka-sensei, a retired high school geometry teacher at Seikyo Gakuen. I met Iisaka-sensei on a cold December afternoon. He wore a red dress shirt, an old green bomber jacket, and a faded baseball cap slanted off the top of his head. Throughout the afternoon, he spoke maybe five times. His eyes would close, just for a moment, and then he'd begin in a slow, raspy voice. More often, his gentle, knowing smile spoke for him.

After thirty-two years at Seikyo Gakuen, Iisaka-sensei began growing strawberries. Not just any strawberries, either. His plants are hydroponic. Instead of the traditional, soil-based approach to growing fruit, Iisaka-sensei uses a high-tech, circuit-like system of water and minerals. All his strawberry beds, tucked inside a humid white greenhouse, sit four feet off the ground.

Iisaka-sensei is impeccably generous. I know his farm so well because I picked almost 150 strawberries in one afternoon. He walked next to me, row by row, placing all the best strawberries into my basket. Every December, he sends twenty jars of homemade strawberry jam across the Pacific to his friends in Carmel. I asked him what makes his strawberries so good. He smiled, and right away I could tell he was thinking of a joke. "Because I grew them," he said.

The teacher in him is still alive and well. Every month, a group of local college students drive up to the farm and listen to him lecture on hydroponic farming and sustainable agriculture. About ten years ago, Iisaka-sensei built a stone oven near the greenhouses to share one of his favorite recipes: a fresh strawberry dessert pizza.

I didn't attend one of his lectures. But I'm sure, like the man himself, they're wise and humble and captivating. I picture Iisaka-sensei saying only one or two words at a time, serving strawberry pizza, and flashing a smile to any student who needs it.

STRAWBERRY PIZZA

STRAWBERRY PIZZA

(Makes 1 large pizza)

INGREDIENTS

For the crust

- 1 pre-made pizza dough
- 1 tablespoon butter, melted
- 1 tablespoon sugar
- 1/2 teaspoon cinnamon

For the topping

- 8 ounces cream cheese, softened
- 1/4 cup powdered sugar
- 1 teaspoon vanilla extract
- 1/2 cup strawberry jam or preserves
- 1 cup fresh strawberries, sliced

INSTRUCTIONS

1. Preheat oven to 375° F (190° C).
2. Roll out pizza dough onto a baking sheet or pizza pan. Brush with melted butter and sprinkle with sugar and cinnamon.
3. Bake for 12-15 minutes or until golden brown. Let cool completely.
4. In a bowl, mix cream cheese, powdered sugar, and vanilla until smooth. Spread over cooled crust.
5. Gently heat strawberry jam and spread a thin layer over the cream cheese.
6. Top with sliced strawberries and garnish with whipped cream or white chocolate if desired.
7. Slice and serve immediately or chill before serving.

SUGAR CREAM PIE

There is one dessert that reigns supreme in Indiana. Like any self-respecting confection, it is not healthy. It is not light. It is, however, delicious. I'm talking about sugar cream pie. Or, as it's sometimes called around the state, Hoosier cream pie.

The pie adheres to a core principle of Indiana's food culture: the best-tasting thing is usually the simplest thing. Think of a fresh slice of watermelon. Sugar cream pie boasts just a handful of ingredients and comes together in the kitchen in about an hour. It's a quick recipe. Its history, however, is over two hundred years old.

Hang with me for a second. Indiana officially became a state in 1816. Due to its rich soil and predictable seasons, the state soon developed a strong reputation for agriculture—one that remains true today. But money and food were scarce at the time. Indiana's Amish community turned to whatever ingredients were around the farm, namely milk, flour, and sugar. Forget fresh peaches— there's a reason sugar cream pie is also called desperation pie. It's not glamorous or even seasonal. But it's a slice of Indiana's Amish history, one almost as old as the state itself.

The pie is sweet—that shouldn't come as a surprise. It's also rich, exceptionally so, with a custard-like texture. A simpler way of saying all this is that the pie lives up to its name. There are no real surprises, no unplaceable flavors, no technical instructions. This is not

Sugar Cream Pie
aka Hoosier Cream Pie
aka Desperation Pie.

Baked Alaska. But maybe that's the whole point: When something this simple tastes this good, it sticks around for two hundred years. And, after trying my first slice, I'm confident it'll be around for two hundred more.

SUGAR CREAM PIE

(Makes 1 pie)

INGREDIENTS

- 1 pie crust
- 4 tbsp. all-purpose flour
- 2 tbsp. cold butter
- 1 cup sugar
- 1 pinch salt
- 1 cup heavy cream
- 1 cup whole milk
- 1 tsp. vanilla extract
- 1/2 tsp. grated nutmeg

Directions

1. Preheat oven to 300° F (148° C)

2. Roll out pie crust and line in 9-inch pie tin

3. Blend flour, butter, sugar, and salt in a food processor until combined and smooth. Pour mixture into pie shell.

4. Add cream into pie mixture and gently mix ingredients with your fingers.

5. Combine milk and vanilla in a measuring cup. Pour, but do not stir, into cream filling. Sprinkle generously with nutmeg.

6. Bake for approx. 90 minutes (center may still be a little wiggly).

7. Cool completely, cut, and serve.

CHRISTMAS CAKE

My first Santa spotting in Kawachinagano occurred on November 10. Not too weird, considering Japan doesn't celebrate Thanksgiving. There are no November inhibitions about celebrating Christmas as soon as the Halloween candy vanishes. But I didn't spot Santa at City Hall or any place you'd expect to find holiday decorations. I was biking past Kentucky Fried Chicken.

I got off my bike and moved closer. Santa sported a silky Van Dyke mustache. No tiny, frameless eyeglasses, either. KFC Santa rocked thick, horn-rimmed frames. This wasn't Mr. Claus, I realized. This was Colonel Sanders, Christmas style.

If you live outside Japan, you probably don't associate KFC with Christmas. The fast-food chain doesn't evoke nostalgia, and you're not fighting to secure drumsticks for your holiday table. But inside the country, Colonel Sanders may as well be Santa Claus. Almost four million families eat KFC for Christmas every year. Scrambling to book a drumstick bucket weeks ahead is just part of the tradition.

But why is "KFC Christmas" a tradition at all? It's thanks to Takeshi Okawara, the manager of Japan's first KFC location. As Okawara tells it, he overheard two foreigners in his shop discussing the lack of Christmas turkeys in Japan. The same night, he woke up from a dream and jotted down the words "party barrel," an idea that eventually became the store's hottest-selling Christmas item. In 1974, KFC launched its "Kentucky for Christmas" ad campaign

CHRISTMAS CAKE

alongside Okawara's party barrel. And the message still sells. To-day, KFC Japan makes around five percent of its yearly revenue on Christmas Eve alone.

I wasn't about to be the only one sitting around on the holidays without fried chicken. I called the Tsunamotos, my first home family in Kawachinagano. They were understandably skeptical about a dinner table full of drumsticks. Still, I think Takeo-san and Ko-to-san sensed my longing for Kentucky for Christmas. We found a compromise: I'd order KFC, they would make "real dinner," and we'd all bake a Christmas cake together.

Kawachinagano in December got cold quickly, and not in the Hallmark card way. Cold in the freezing windchill, can't-feel-my-face way. Huddled by the portable heater in the kitchen, Takeo-san and I could hear the wind whipping off the side walls. My phone buzzed. Our KFC order was ready for pickup. We locked eyes, bracing for the walk outside to the family car. Then, we nodded. Takeo-san grabbed his leather jacket, I laced up my boots, and we set off along the empty streets to KFC.

The whole marketing campaign, as is often the case, was better than the product itself. Christmas chicken was just . . . chicken. It looked silly next to the Tsunamoto family's spread. I conveyed my remorse by eating an amount of salad, sashimi, and white rice that can only be described as apologetic. I brought presents, too, which helped my case.

Japan's other Christmas tradition—the one without Santa-clad colonels—is Christmas cake. It's a simple dessert: sponge cake finished with whipped cream, topped with strawberries, and decorated with chocolate. Christmas cake (*kurisumasu keki* in Japanese) first appeared in Tokyo pastry shops around 1910. The tradition quickly spread around the country, like a nationwide craving for strawberry shortcake.

Koto-san planned ahead, baking the sponge cake while Takeo-san and I dispatched to KFC. We all gathered back in the kitchen after dinner to decorate our cake. Takeo-san, our resident artist, took the creative approach. A strawberry here, a chocolate there. We placed pretzel sticks around the top until we had a full snowman. "MERRY CRISTMAS," the final product read. I'll fully admit that I ate the candy *H* during the icing process. Strictly research, of course.

CHRISTMAS CAKE

(Makes one 6-inch cake)

INGREDIENTS

Sponge cake

- ○ 3 eggs
- ○ 1/2 cup (100g) sugar
- ○ 3/4 cup (90g) cake flour, sifted
- ○ 1 tablespoon milk
- ○ 1 tablespoon unsalted butter, melted
- ○ 1/2 teaspoon vanilla extract

Whipped cream Frosting

- ○ 1 cup (240ml) heavy cream
- ○ 2 tablespoons sugar
- ○ 1/2 teaspoon vanilla extract

Decoration

- ○ 1 cup fresh strawberries, hulled and sliced
  (plus whole ones for topping)
- ○ 2 tablespoons strawberry jam (optional)

INSTRUCTIONS

① Preheat the oven to 350° F (175° c). Grease and line a 6-inch round cake pan with parchment paper.

② In a mixing bowl, whisk the eggs and sugar over a double boiler until the mixture is warm. Remove from heat and beat on high speed for about five minutes until light and fluffy.

③ Gently fold in the sifted cake flour. Add the melted butter, milk, and vanilla extract, folding until just combined.

④ Pour the batter into the prepared pan and bake for 20-25 minutes, or until a toothpick inserted into the center comes out clean. Let the cake cool completely.

⑤ To prepare the whipped cream, beat the heavy cream, sugar, and vanilla extract until stiff peaks form.

⑥ Once the sponge cake has cooled, slice it in half horizontally. Spread a thin layer of whipped cream over the bottom layer, then add a layer of sliced strawberries. If using, spread a thin layer of strawberry jam.

⑦ Place the second sponge layer on top and cover the entire cake with the remaining whipped cream.

⑧ Decorate with whole strawberries arranged on top. For a festive touch, lightly dust the strawberries with powdered sugar.

⑨ Refrigerate for at least one hour before serving.

BANANA CREAM CAKE

There's a saying on the Cake Bake Shop's website that hints at the company's wider success. It's a quote by Walt Disney executive Marty Sklar, the man who designed countless Disney parks and resorts around the world. "Dream it, do it," he says.

Sklar's saying, posted alongside a portrait of Cake Bake Shop's founder and owner, Gwendolyn Rogers, is fitting. The story of Rogers' success reads like a fairytale of its own.

Of course, the success didn't come overnight. Rogers didn't make Oprah's "Favorite Things" list just because she bakes nice cakes. Cake Bake Shop's fame is the latent measure of her relentless dedication—over fifty years of dedication, actually, and a lot of cake batter.

Rogers started baking as a six-year-old growing up in Sun Valley, Idaho. But this wasn't some feel-good childhood. At thirteen, she got her first job cleaning floors at the movie theater. When that ended, she bounced between restaurants, first as a prep cook, then as a dishwasher, and finally as a waitress. The jobs started to blur together. Her love for baking, however, remained clear.

She eventually went off to college, married, and moved back to Idaho to raise three boys. But when the family moved to Indianapolis, Rogers felt helpless. Her life in Sun Valley was thousands of miles away. Almost instinctively, she reached for the things that saved her as a teen: sugar, flour, eggs, and butter. Rogers built cakes with a new energy. She soon leaned into life as a full-time baker in Indianapolis.

The Cake Bake Shop didn't start there, though. Rogers' dream was alive, but she needed the chance to prove it. Finally, after eight years of baking in her kitchen and searching for retail investors, she got her shot: a $300,000, 3-year loan. Rogers took the risk and opened the Cake Bake Shop in 2014 on Carrollton Avenue in northern Indianapolis. The fairytale was alive, even if just barely.

Her location took off almost immediately. The thirty-person dining room that once felt enormous couldn't keep up with the new wave of reservations. Rogers paid back the loan and quickly started shopping for a second location. This time, she found what she needed in Carmel.

In 2019, Rogers opened the Cake Bake Shop's second location in the Carmel City Center. The new shop is a testament to Marty Sklar's "dream it, do it" mindset. The interior is 4,500 square feet of fairytale: pristine whites, ivy greens, and hints of pink engulfing room after room of velvet, diamond, and marble. It's a place for celebration—which is good, because securing a reservation at the 150-seat bakery and restaurant is worth celebrating in itself.

And then, finally, there are the cakes. Rogers' cakes aren't trying to shock or stand out. In fact, many of them look familiar. But all familiarity fades with the first bite. Each slice, whether Black Forest, red velvet, or award-winning chocolate, is rich, moist, and unbelievably delicious. But that's just how Rogers does things. In her kitchen, fairy tales come to life.

BANANA CREAM CAKE

(Makes one 8-inch, 4-layer cake)

For the cake

- 2 1/2 cups all-purpose flour
- 1 tablespoon baking powder
- 1/2 teaspoon fine sea salt
- 3/4 cup (1 1/2 sticks) unsalted butter, room temperature
- 2 1/2 cups sugar, divided
- 6 large eggs
- 1 cup plus 2 tablespoons buttermilk
- 2 small ripe bananas, diced (about 1 ½ cups)

For the Banana caramel cream

- 1 1/2 cups packed golden brown sugar
- 1 small ripe banana, cut into 1-inch pieces
- 3 tablespoons unsalted butter, room temperature
- 3 3/4 cups chilled heavy cream, divided
- 4 1/2 teaspoons fresh lime juice, divided
- 4 1/2 teaspoons dark rum, divided

For the Sea Salt Roasted Pecans

- 2 cups pecan halves
- 3 tablespoons unsalted butter, melted
- 1 1/4 teaspoons fine sea salt

① Preheat oven to 325° F. Toss pecans with melted butter and salt, then spread on a baking sheet. Bake for 15 minutes, until fragrant. Cool completely.

② Preheat oven to 350° F. Grease and flour two 9-inch cake pans.

③ Whisk together flour, baking powder, and salt. In a large bowl, beat butter and 1 cup sugar until smooth. Add 2 eggs and mix well. Alternate adding dry ingredients and buttermilk, starting and ending with dry.

④ In a separate bowl, beat the remaining 4 eggs and 1 1/2 cups sugar until pale and thick, about 4 minutes. Fold into the batter along with the diced bananas. Divide batter evenly between pans.

⑤ Bake for 35 minutes. Let cool for 15 minutes, then turn out onto wire racks to cool completely.

⑥ Blend brown sugar, banana, and butter until smooth. Add 1 1/2 cups cream and blend again. Transfer to a saucepan and bring to a boil, stirring occasionally. Cook without stirring until caramel reaches 218° F. Cool to room temperature.

⑦ Whip the remaining 2 1/4 cups heavy cream until soft peaks form. Gradually fold in the cooled caramel. Chill until firm, about 3 hours.

⑧ Slice each cake in half to create four layers. Place one layer on a platter and drizzle with 1 1/2 teaspoons lime juice and 1 1/4 teaspoons rum. Spread with 1 1/4 cups caramel cream. Repeat for the next two layers.

⑨ Place the final layer on top, cut side down. Spread the remaining caramel cream over the cake. Top with roasted pecans. Refrigerate until ready to serve.

SAKÉ

Exit the train at Kawachinagano Station and walk south until you find a narrow, sloping road called Kōya Kaido. You'll know it when you see it. The Kōya Kaido is a historic pilgrimage route between Kyoto, Osaka, and Mount Kōya in Wakayama. Its winding path cuts straight through Kawachinagano's city center, like a distant cousin of Carmel's Monon Trail. The shops and houses lining the Kōya Kaido share its history. Traditional wooden facades, covered by dark, slate-tile roofs, peak out around each turn.

One building stands out against the rest. It's not particularly flashy or looming, but it embodies the type of authority that can't be bought overnight. There are details, too, small things that hint at the building's lore. The surrounding block, grazing the Kōya Kaido's gentle curves, is spotlessly clean. The exterior wooden siding, stretched to cover the first floor of the two-floor building, is a shade of aged, dark brown. Perhaps most obviously, a ball of pine needles hangs under the entryway like an evergreen holiday ornament.

This is Amanosake, the oldest saké brewery in Kawachinagano. And the cedar ornament is a sugidama, the annual sign that new saké is ready.

Throughout the winter, I kept hearing that Amanosake's new saké was almost ready. Their website was updating. Piles of cedar started

And then there are the details,
Small things that hint at the
building's lore.

Sugidama

forming in the parking lot.
The Kōya Kaido was stirring.

The new saké ceremony arrived early on the morning of November 24, before any sunlight could break onto the shivering crowd assembled outside. I was half awake, secretly wishing we'd be drinking coffee, not saké. But, despite my frozen fingers and five hours of sleep, I couldn't stop thinking about the ritual's history. Amanosake has been crafting saké in Kawachinagano since 1718 AD. The family is in its tenth generation of ownership. There's a special type of reverence, I decided, that one should extend to businesses and buildings older than one's own country.

Yozo Saijo, the founder's great-great-great-great-great-great-great-grandson, thanked us for showing up in the cold. He retrieved a small ladder, climbed up to the dark green *sugidama*, and poured a fresh bottle of saké through the top of the ornament. We clapped as the saké splashed down the branches. I can't pretend I understood the full significance of the moment. But the crowd seemed satisfied, the sun was finally out, and the staff were delivering trays of fresh saké. There are worse ways to conclude a ceremony.

Amanosake's saké tasted sweet and clean, with a deceptively smooth aftertaste for 16 percent alcohol content. Like most saké, it was a mix of rice, rice-malt, and water. While water makes up almost 80 percent of the alcohol, rice is the star ingredient. More specifically, *shuzo-kotekimai* (literally "rice suitable for brewing saké").

Amanosake brews a variety of saké from these base ingredients. There is the cold *ginjo-shu*, the hot *junmai-shu*, and the cloudy-white nigorizake, along with countless variations of temperature, color, and strength. It's a lot to memorize—daunting but worthwhile. If you're short on time, here's the crash course: Just choose one. They all taste great. And cheers in Japanese is *kampai*.

ACKNOWLEDGEMENTS

This book simply would not exist without the support of the Kawachinagano International Friendship Association (KIFA). I am so grateful for KIFA's guidance before, during, and after my visit to Osaka in 2022. Shiba-san, Yamamoto-san, Goto-san, Megumi-san, Hiroko-san, Yoshie-san, Ueda-san, and Yuki-san, thank you for showing me what it really means to be a sister city.

Throughout my writing, I received incredible support from government offices in Carmel and Kawachinagano. Former Mayor Jim Brainard believed in this project back at the beginning in February 2022. Mayor Sue Finkam and her team, especially Andris Berzins and Rebecca Carl, continued that legacy, providing crucial support during this book's editing and publication phases. In Kawachinagano, Former Mayor Tomoaki Shimada welcomed me to his city with no hesitation. As did Higashi-san.

I'm so thankful to KIFA for arranging several homestays during my trip. Thank you to the Yamazakis and Gary Luscombe for opening your doors to me. Nanten-en is, without a doubt, the most special inn I've ever visited. And I give my undying gratitude to the Miyazakis and Tsunamotos. Your families are my family now.

I owe the members of Carmel's sister city network a massive thanks for entrusting me with the relationships they built over the past thirty years. Mindy Linn nudged me down the right path countless times. Barb Moshier is a giant of the Carmel-Kawachinagano relationship; we're all standing on her shoulders today. And nothing would have happened without Evan Kreutzer's leadership. In Japan, I routinely received more credit than I was due simply because I knew them.

Theresa Kulczak, the Japan-America Society of Indiana (JASI), and the wider Indiana-Japan community could not have been more supportive throughout my research. Theresa's work with JASI is consistently excellent, as are her colleagues, Minori Abel and Jeremiah Maxwell. I also want to thank Larry Ingraham stateside and Paul Roland in Tokyo.

My success is a product of the people in my life, starting with my parents and sisters. Thank you for moving our family group chat to WhatsApp. Many friends saw variations of this book and provided helpful feedback. I am deeply grateful to the following people: Ryan Van Slyke, Anthony Edwards, Lila Simchen, Jay Natarajan, Jingjing Xiao, Joe Killion, Callum Thomas, Chrissy Cutting, Shakeel Zia, Amanda Cassano, and Greta Gevorgyan. And I owe everything to Pearl McAndrews, my first and longest-running editor. Love you.

I would not have wanted to create this book without Takeo Tsunamoto. I still can't believe my words get to share the page with his illustrations.

Lastly, I want to thank all of the local businesses and individuals featured in the book's chapters. Your food continues to tell the story of our cities.

www.ingramcontent.com/pod-product-compliance
Lightning Source LLC
Chambersburg PA
CBHW071350280326
41927CB00040B/2587